BUILD A BUSINESS WITH GUSTO

ATTRACTING STRATEGIC INVESTORS TO FUND YOUR VISION

GREG WEISS

Difference Press

Washington, DC, USA

Published 2023

DISCLAIMER

Editing: Madeline Kosten

Cover design: Jennifer Stimson

Author photo courtesy of: the Photografix team

CONTENTS

To my family

ATTRACTING SMART MONEY

It was a beautiful Saturday morning when I met up for the first time with a guy named Chris. We'd been set up by a mutual friend who thought I might be the one to help Chris fund his dream. I remember sitting back and noticing I hardly touched my cappuccino, not because it was bad, but because Chris's enthusiasm reminded me of a child on Christmas Day who can't wait to open up his presents. As I listened, I could see his passion for wanting more, being more, and even wanting to belong. I could see that our conversation played out many times in his head before, and would not have been surprised if this was not the first time he was having this conversation. Chris had thought this through many times before, and in his mind, he had done his due diligence. Now, all he had to do was convince someone, anyone, to give him the money, and they would both make a killing – I mean, why wouldn't they just give him some money? His story was convincing, and he convinced himself that there was lots of money to be made.

Now Chris deserved to get a break; he comes from a working-class family and had worked hard all his life, which was not only sunshine and roses for him. His story was so familiar and not only resonated with me as a person but also with many others I had the privilege to listen to before. He so desperately wanted to be a success and increase his self-worth and the worth of others around him. If he could only create a successful business, his dreams would come true. He was ready to go the distance and, in his mind, eliminate all the risks, so the only outcome had to be success.

I was Chris once.

It was looking back and I could feel the emotional connection I was building with him. I could feel my eagerness growing, the desire to help the old me sitting in front of me. If only I knew back then what I know today, my conversation, like what Chris had with me, would have been so much easier. I probably would not have made so many mistakes in business and in life. The mistakes Chris was about to make – and the ones I made – were not different than the mistakes any of us make. I did not want to take Chris's opportunity to learn from his mistakes away from him, but I also know that you can learn just as much from other people's mistakes as your own, so why not skip that process completely?

Why can't Chris learn from my mistakes and my successes without me?

I truly wanted him to succeed, not to please me or

even to please him, but because I believe we all deserve a chance in life, and those who step up and go for it should have a fighting chance. However, most new entrepreneurs, like Chris, don't really have a fair chance because they lack the one thing that matters most: perspective.

Chris doesn't know this yet, but he does not just need money; he also needs a mentor – a person invested in him as a person who wants to see him succeed not only in business but also in life. Many visionaries think they can do it themselves and that if someone will just take a chance on them and give them money, they can help everyone get rich. Business rarely works this way. To be stronger, we all need others, even if we don't think so; this does not make us weak or desperate, it makes us human.

I have not always wanted to be in business, I just wanted to be more and better than who I was in the past. I have not always lived life with gusto, and life has thrown many obstacles in my way, so that's why I resonate with Chris and others I listen to.

That day over coffee, Chris came wanting to find someone with plenty of cash and a deep rolodex to fund his dream and make some key intros. He thought what he had to offer – a great idea, passion, and the chance for both of us to be basically printing cash, would be enough – *should* be enough. What Chris left with was a choice. The same choice I'll leave you with at the end of this book should you make it to the end.

I told Chris he had to decide if he wanted dumb money or smart money. Dumb money leaves you on your own to try to figure everything out. Dumb money can look like a great deal if you don't know the true cost. Dumb money means it's all on you. This kind of money can be hard or easy to find. It can be loans or GoFundMe campaigns or even an inheritance, but it's expensive money because you will use it to basically buy lottery tickets.

Smart money is harder to get and comes with more strings. Smart money is about building long-term relationships and trust. Smart money increases your chance of success exponentially, but it also means you can't do everything your way. It's a partnership, and partnership means compromise – hopefully, the type that makes you both a whole lot richer.

In this book, you will learn what it takes to get that smart money from a strategic partner who is excited to fund your project and to mentor you along the way. You will learn how to be the person a "rich guy" might want to back. I believe you deserve that chance, just like I believed Chris did. To be the person who gets that chance, you have to decide:

Are you willing to become the person who can attract the smart money?

IDEAS ARE EASY

You don't have to search far to get advice; I mean, sometimes the neighbour has it all figured out. Some will advise from a position of authority or from textbooks. If they made it, you will as well, right? I mean, if the textbook says so, why should it not be true?

People should not just be told what to do, they should be invested in the philosophy, "I do not talk about money but instead of time and one's knowledge."

You need time and knowledge of what your business or venture really stands for. You need to be shaped and crafted to understand what it is that really is going to make your business tick and why others should take notice and want to be part of it. You want to have a strategic partner who wants you to succeed.

For others to know what you want out of business, you need to know yourself. You need to be aware of why you want to go on this venture in the first place. So, what does success look like to you? Do you just want to be your own boss so that you do not have to worry about someone looking over your shoulder? Do you want to substitute or subsidise your income and lifestyle just to a comfortable level, or do you want to build a skyscraper business towering into the clouds? You might even just be happy enough to build a retirement plan through a business asset. Whatever it is that you want, you need to know so that you can manage your own expectations and those of others.

Your journey will go through a mountain range; there will be some steep climbs to take, and there will be some easy descents, but when the sunlight hits your face at the top, it is all worth it. I can still feel the struggles and pain of my life journey, and I feel that same emotion with my peers, family, and the people I build business relationships with.

To find a strategic investor, it's not just about having the right connections or who you know. It's about how you present yourself and your business and what you are willing to put in to make it work. You have to show intent and not wait for others to do the work for you. There's a wealth of information available to you today to show that you have thought this through and have a business mindset. You also have to show you have taken some risks and that you've invested in the idea. Demonstrate that you have done some meaningful research through competitive analysis. Make your vision tangible by presenting a prototype of the product. Share your experience and knowledge base and eagerness to learn more. If you are an accountant and you want to open a coffee shop, then spending six months as a part-time assistant manager at a local shop can show that you are learning about this new industry.

TWO TYPES OF SMART MONEY BUSINESSES

There are two types of businesses that are ripe for strategic investment:

- Businesses that fully understand their value proposition but need to know how to execute it more efficiently. How can the business reach more people or diversify its communication channels?
- Businesses that have a good value proposition but need financial or industry expertise to make it better.

If you just want a lifestyle business, you aren't going to get an investor because there isn't a return. Investors don't want to fund your lifestyle. They do not want to spend charity money; they want to spend strategic money. You will want to have a business that can do both. You can have the best business proposal known to mankind, but if it only creates value for you, a loan will be your best option.

You will only have one opportunity to reach out to a strategic investor, and if you reach out too soon, you have every chance of not being able to convince others to part with their strategic money or even set up a follow-up meeting.

Do not reach out if you don't understand how much money you will need and what you will need it for. Most people don't understand their cash requirements, and you also need to have a good reason for wanting an investment. If you just want cash to buy time or to sustain your business, the funding will be hard to get. You need to have a strategic reason that the cash is strategic and will solve a problem that *creates* value, not just keep your creditors away for a few months.

"I need to buy good inventory because the incremental growth is faster than my cash flow can sustain" is better than "I need money to pay my bills because I'm behind on my supplies." Investors aren't interested in buying a Band-Aid to fix a problem but not the cause.

BETTING ON THE SMART MONEY

Imagine what it would feel like if you could build the business you are dreaming of, bringing it to the level. You look in the mirror, and you feel amazing that you set out and accomplished what you always wanted to. Maybe you would have material things like a second house or car or motorcycle, but more than that, you would know your family was safe, and you would be able to support them if anything happened. And even better, you would know that you had proven everyone who ever doubted you wrong. This is possible in any scenario, but with a strategic investor, your odds of success go way up. With someone on your side who has the experience you don't and the money you need, this dream will be in focus and ready for you to claim.

To set yourself up for speedy success, you need to eliminate the tedious process most strategic investors have to go through. The sooner they know what they will be investing in, the sooner they will part with their smart money. Investors are looking to understand your cost factors and do not want any surprises. Instead, they want clarity on all your revenue streams, current and potential. What's your value proposition and how do you create this through the supply chain, and who is the target market and the size of the prize?

Only when you can talk intelligently about these things are you ready to talk to an investor, and that is the conversation this book is going to prepare you to have in a meaningful and productive way.

That is what you are going to learn in this book: how to be the person who attracts the smart money. I hope you are ready for this because you are in for a ride.

2

SMALL TOWN RUGBY PLAYER
WITH BIG DREAMS

I graduated from secondary school in 1999. I had dreams of moving on to bigger things and leaving the comfortable confines of everything I had known up until that point. My sights were set on becoming a sports psychologist. I've always had a passion for people and always wanted to help. I got introduced to sports psychology through my own experience in athletics and playing rugby from a very young age. Sports psychology seemed like the perfect fusion of my interests in athletics and the human mind.

I did my first years of studies and got promised sponsorships from various local businesses from my local town through various interactive sports teams. Unfortunately, when it came time actually to pay for tuition and expenses, those promises materialized into little real funding, and I was unable to get my first year's results to advance to the second year. Growing up poor and needing financial help in the first place, I had no means to pay those outstanding amounts.

TAKING A LEAP OF FAITH

I decided to work for one year to pay off all my debt to university and then start studying again and try and complete it.

I managed to get work as a receptionist at a Dulux paint store. I got the opportunity through a rugby team-mate whose family owned the store in my local town. During this time, I stayed with my aunt to reduce living costs, but it still was not really enough to pay off all my debt to the university.

But as human nature will have it, once you leave university and you start earning money, it's very hard to leave that set of life and get back into the steady way of doing things, especially when you take care of yourself.

My friend from high school's father bought a paint shop in a city called Pretoria in South Africa. Because of my experience and training in paint sales, they offered me a sales rep position.

I decided to move to Pretoria in South Africa at the age of twenty. When I moved, it was the first time I would actually stay on my own accord. I managed to find a small flat which was actually a house cleaner's quarters behind a house.

It had a single bedroom and a very small kitchen. I remember with my very first salary, I actually bought myself a fridge and actually slept on a mattress on the floor as I couldn't afford a bed at that point in time.

During this time, I also joined a rugby league team in South Africa.

I managed to get into the First Division team at a

young age, and by this team assessment, I was able to do it in Russia.

I played some rugby in Russia and got valuable experience of teamwork and camaraderie, but also an understanding of new ethnicities and cultures that really opened my eyes as to how big the world really is out there.

During this time, I stayed in Pretoria, which was also known as the university town. Even though I wasn't attending the university at that point in time, I was enjoying the student life. I got all the student perks, and it was actually a very exciting time. I used this time to really start to unwind a little bit and enjoy the type of freedom a university student would have enjoyed without the pressure of having to study at the same time.

OPEN DOORS

Once again, through one of my old rugby teammates from my hometown, I had an opportunity to join a food distribution sales company. The trick, though, was that I would work on a 1-percent commission only. In a sense, I was subcontracting to the business, and this was my first exposure to running a business, although I did not perceive it that way then. Knowing how well he was doing, I took a leap of faith and decided to take on the risk.

It turned out that I actually happened to be good at sales! By age twenty-two, I was earning great money, which was new to me, having grown up without much.

I enjoyed the freedom of disposable income and built a lifestyle to match, buying nice cars and clothes.

Not growing up with money, I enjoyed this new sense of having money and needless to say spoiled myself a lot. I adopted this persona that I had to have the best to prove my worth and bought the best cars and the nicest clothes. I still considered some investment mindset and bought my first property, and by the age of twenty-five, I had three cars and three properties.

BLINDSIDED BY BUSINESS REALITIES

After a few years of riding high in sales, the tides turned abruptly. The food distribution company lost some major supplier contracts, which significantly reduced inventory. Almost overnight, my income dropped by 75 percent due to lower sales volume. I quickly realised I had been living well beyond sustainable means.

Without proper business acumen and reserves, I was unable to maintain my lavish lifestyle in light of this drastic income reduction. I was still saddled with significant debts I had taken on during more flush times, thinking the steady commissions would continue rolling in indefinitely. I was forced to declare liquidation, which was devastating professionally and personally.

At twenty-five, everything I had worked hard to attain – the properties, cars, reputation – was gone in an instant. It was a very humbling low point. I was left wondering how I could recover from this monumental setback. With no place to stay amidst this crisis, a close friend, Louis, and his fiancée, Talita, benevolently offered up their couch temporarily until I got back on my feet.

It's during the darkest hours that beams of light emerge. My friend's fiancée happened to work for a food distribution wholesaler, which had a new opening well aligned with my sales background and people skills. She believed in me enough to submit my resume and land me an interview during a very unstable chapter. Her compassionate intervention led to a job offer, which gave me a path forward. I was the youngest Business Development Manager the company had at that point in time, and this experience rebuilt me both financially and personally.

Looking back, I learnt early on through rugby about the power of connections. Team sports inherently provide access to people from all walks of life that you may never otherwise cross paths with. I discovered that who you know often matters more than what you know when it comes to getting a foot in the door. Your network is an extension of you – friends of friends can morph into job leads and business partners over time, even if you haven't met them directly. A personal reference short circuits the tedious process of applications and interviews.

The connections I made on the rugby pitch came full circle, ultimately helping resurrect my career after liquidation. I learnt to appreciate how naturally forming bonds and relationships can plant seeds for future mutual benefit. A little generosity and human connection go a long way.

FINDING MY CALLING

After the food wholesale industry took a chance on me, I spent the next fifteen years working my way up, eventually overseeing national accounts. Our core business was supplying independent grocery store owners with various food and beverage products they would then sell to consumers locally.

This became my core competency – interfacing directly with and advising business owners versus just pushing products. My role focused on collaborating with clients to help grow and optimise their businesses holistically, not just make sales quotas. I found the challenge deeply fulfilling, rebuilding my career from the ground up in an industry I had not envisioned entering. Hard work and nurturing relationships led to consistency and stability, redeeming my reputation after past missteps. I will never forget the joy I felt when I was able to qualify for a phone contract after my liquidation. I never realised how valuable it is to have your name back and not be blacklisted. My experiences made me wiser and more restrained, though still with an appetite for smart risks.

AMBITIOUS BUT ILL-TIMED VENTURE

My wife and I were working for a laser hair removal company that solely specialised in laser hair removal. I knew the owner, and he approached me and asked if we would be interested in buying the business. After spending over a decade learning the wholesale distribution world, I was ready to parlay my skills into an entrepreneurial endeavour. I had an appetite for smart risks and hoped to build something of my own. The offer was for us to buy his company for a nominal $1 fee. My wife and I couldn't say no. The deal was too good to good to be true. The pitch was enticing – we would take over the existing client contracts and lease with limited upfront investment. Their business model relied on selling prepaid discount package deals to clients upfront. Given my sales background, I was confident I could optimise operations.

In addition to honouring the prepaid packages, my value-add would be expanding the services offered beyond just laser hair removal to include things like facials, massage, microdermabrasion, and other ancillary aesthetics treatments. I aimed to upsell existing customers these new services while also tapping into a wider market by broadening our offering.

In the first six months, we tripled the company's historical revenues as existing customers converted to higher-priced packages and new clientele came aboard. But the surge in sales proved deceiving. While revenue rose sharply, our fixed overhead costs outpaced the gains. The core of our sales still stemmed from prepaid discount packages that had razor-thin margins. My lofty assumptions that customers would purchase more proved to be flawed.

Then, I found myself at another crossroads in my personal life. I was the eldest of three brothers. My second eldest brother was born with brain damage and was disabled for his entire life. He passed away in 2004 due to heart failure. But on April 8th, 2010, my youngest brother died in a car crash on my mother's birthday.

Amidst the personal tragedy, two hard-fought years after opening my business later, it was clear the venture would end in financial turmoil if I persisted in trying to make the flawed model work. My previous liquidation still haunted me. Shutting down an enterprise you poured blood, sweat, and tears into is never easy, but the sting is far less severe than owing debts you cannot repay. I managed to sell the business in the same manner as we bought it, but with an already increased turnover and a more cash-flush investor, they were better set up for success when I was at the point when we bought it.

The loss in my business life and the loss of both of my brothers profoundly impacted me. It made me realise that tomorrow is promised to no one. Almost like a switch flipped in my mindset, I set out to live as productively as possible and seize each day with gusto.

Two months later, I proposed to my beautiful wife, Lecinda, and we got married on December 16, 2011, the following year. I decided I had put off pursuing my studies for too long and enrolled in my first business diploma program in August 2010. I figured that if I was going back to school, I may as well continue all the way to a master's degree. So, in 2012, I began part-time studies for an MBA at the University of Stellenbosch Business School. Studying part-time allowed me to still provide for my wife while furthering my education. I finally graduated with an MBA in 2015.

On September 26th, my life changed again – my wife and I were blessed with the birth of our beautiful daughter, Miané. After the stinging failure of my entrepreneurial venture and tragically losing both my brothers, I found myself at a crossroads. Financially and emotionally devastated, everything felt uncertain. But the arrival of our baby girl Miané gave me new purpose and joy. Though juggling the demands of a new family, career turmoil, and delayed studies tested me tremendously, their unwavering love and support gave me the strength to persevere. My wife and daughter were my inspiration to build a better life for our family. I realised I had been given a second chance, and I was determined to chart a course out of South Africa and off to somewhere new. But where?

CHARTING A COURSE FOR NEW HORIZONS

The world is becoming smaller as business is becoming increasingly global. I understood that being exposed to new economies and lifestyles for my family was an idea I had to explore. My father lives in Perth, Australia, so Australia was at the top of our list. I applied for a skilled worker visa and was planning for our imminent move. But my initial skills assessment was rejected, which was devastating at first. However, when a goal becomes a must, I knew there was no alternative but to try again.

My wife identified a different skill I could apply under, and this time I secured approval. With immigration now confirmed, I applied for the General Manager of Merchandise and Marketing role at the biggest independent supermarket retail group in Australia before departing. But I was declined due to lacking local industry knowledge. When I first moved alone, my family stayed behind temporarily. The plan was for me to get established with work first, as I could handle the rugged start with our limited remaining funds after paying for applications and draining savings. I applied widely, but my lack of Australian market experience proved to be my Achilles' heel initially. I stayed with a family whose daughter worked at KPMG and had recruiter connections. She passed my resume along, which found its way to the same recruiter for the role I had been rejected for.

Knowing I was now in Australia, she set up an interview, and two weeks later, I was hired at the biggest independent supermarket retail group, a South Australian chain brand overseeing 125 stores comprised of thirty-five multi-store operators. This supermarket retail group is known as the premier independent grocer, so this marked my transition from wholesale into supermarkets and closer to the end consumer. I leveraged my business model experience to showcase various avenues for value creation. After working at the biggest independent supermarket retail group in South Australia for two years, I gained experience with some of the highest calibre stores in the country.

LEVERAGING MY KNOWLEDGE

Drawing on all my experience gained in the wholesale industry and my newer expertise in Australian supermarkets, I soon realised there was an opportunity in Queensland, Australia. I still had a strong relationship with my previous company, especially with the Managing Director, Dustin. We discussed the prospect, and with Dustin also contemplating immigration to Australia, we embarked on a new venture together. We created D&G Dream Investments with shareholders in South Africa and began strategically investing in supermarkets since that was our area of expertise.

This new job exposed me to the consumer experience in a way my wholesale supplier role did not. It was the opposite side of the supply chain, putting me directly in front of the end consumer. This further broadened my perspective into deeper aspects of the retail chain and customer priorities. Working for a national supermarket chain provided eye-opening insights compared to my wholesale background. I gained a front-line consumer perspective, which enriched my knowledge substantially. Our model was to focus on quality and shopping experience like no other, and this proved to set us apart in the industry.

I realised the wholesale approach I knew well could disrupt the supermarket industry in Australia the way it had in South Africa.

I collaborated with a trusted South African colleague to make this vision a reality. We both aimed to emigrate, so it was fortuitous timing and an ideal partnership.

Given our core competency in food retail, we began strategically acquiring and revamping supermarkets using an innovative wholesale management model. Over four years, we bought and successfully turned around eleven stores through investors equity and creative problem-solving when inevitable surprises arose.

I was hands-on in developing our unique market positioning to deliver quality and value beyond typical grocery chains. I managed and designed the look and feel of all the stores and created marketing platforms our 30,000-plus weekly emails drove unprecedented customer engagement based on the relationships I had honed over decades in the industry. Opportunity emerges when preparation meets luck. My breadth of expertise allowed me to recognise the potential in Australia and execute despite inherent risks.

BUSINESS RECLAIMED

After selling my stake in the successful supermarket enterprise in June 2023, I came full circle, ready to build something of my own from the ground up again. I launched Live Life with Gusto, a family business aimed at creating multiple revenue streams. However, we would always stay true to my passion and knowledge base in food retail as the foundation.

W'Gusto Supermarkets was born as the inaugural endeavour – a chain where we could wholly control the brand ethos and consumer experience from start to finish. The first store is slated to open in May 2024, with two more on the way and plans to aggressively expand. It's personally fulfilling to create jobs and community value after three decades of observing the industry at large.

My extensive hands-on experience enabled me to start mentoring other entrepreneurs and companies at this stage of my career – investing time back into up-and-comers as others had done for me. I'm currently advising several other startups on strategic planning, which inspired me to write this book and share my playbook on how to find a strategic partner and investor.

It's immensely satisfying to reflect on the past twenty-five years of passion and perseverance. My circuitous path has equipped me with hard-earned wisdom to forge ahead wisely. Though there are inevitable missteps, the shared journey makes us all stronger. I aim to live with gusto while creating enduring value.

3

BUILD A BUSINESS WITH GUSTO FRAMEWORK

When my brother died, I started to live by the philosophy, "Tomorrow is promised to no one so live your life with gusto." As I have lived that commitment, I started to realise two other things.

Everything I teach comes back to "do not create something with just you in mind."

If you help enough people to get what they want, you will get what you want. Live your life with purpose and add value to yourself and others around you.

Close to home, my wife wanted to set up an online business to keep herself busy and potentially be able to turn it into a profitable business, so she started learning how to set up an online store similar to an Etsy. I was happy to be supporting her as she did this, and never once did I think, "if I am paying the bills while she isn't working, I better get something out of it." It was a partnership, and I wasn't thinking about what I was getting. She had a need to create self-worth, and I was able to provide her with a landscape and environment conducive for this. But as it happens, the skills she learnt are amazing for an author and businessperson setting up a new business. Now she does all my marketing for all my businesses, from creating and setting up websites to creating and managing social media platforms, and she is great at it. Not because I wanted something but because it was a true partnership. Almost most of my personal business interests started from me spending time with individuals seeking help. I never go into a meeting with the mindset of helping someone for personal gain.

This is what business partnerships can be like too, when you approach each relationship with a long-term mindset instead of being transactional. As I thought about it more, I started to create the 7 Principles of the Build a Business with Gusto framework, which I want to share here in this book. The 7 principles are simple, but that doesn't make them easy to live.

Here's a quick overview:

1. **Know your value:** Strategic investors follow strategic people, and knowing your value gives you a tradeable asset in exchange for this smart money.

2. **Know what kind of investor you need:** There are multiple avenues for getting money. You can get it from savings, personal loans, or two types of investors, the silent one and the strategist. But money only becomes strategic when it comes to knowledge input

as well. Strategic investors don't just want a return, they want a long-term sustainable relationship.

3. **Know your customer:** True value is the value as perceived by the consumer. You can create the best value offer on the market, but if your target customers do not perceive that as value, you have missed the mark. Value is created when needs are met. So, what are your customer's needs?

4. **Know how to be a good customer:** Modern business models only show one direction of flow of the value chain: supplier to customer, but in fact, every supplier in the channel was a customer to the supplier before him. Understand that as a supplier, you are a customer as well, and building a mutual relationship as a customer will help you to become a better supplier.

5. **Know how to focus on the right activities and track your progress:** When you are a quarterback on an NFL team, you don't focus on your kicking. It won't add value, so you practice your throw and narrow down hitting the target. Understand the drivers that create your value to help you zone in on the key activities needed to perform.

6. **Know how to optimise your cost structure:** Understanding the key cost drivers helps you to identify what can be saved and what needs to change. Cheapest is not always best; it's a

balance between current money investment and long-term savings,

7. **Know how to create solid backup plans:** Do you have a lifeboat for your business? The only constant in life is change, so the question is: are you ready for it?

HOW TO READ THIS BOOK

This book is the culmination of decades of experience on the rugby field and in the business arena. There have been wins and losses, highs and lows, ups and downs. Through it all, there have been many mistakes made that I wish I could do differently. That's why I decided to distil what wisdom I might have earned through the decades here. That said, most readers won't be able to absorb it all on the first read. It might take a few reads to really process what I'm trying to share. My best advice is to read it through once, knowing that some concepts will be lost, but keep the book as a reference, revisiting each of these steps when you get stuck. I'm going to share the Building a Business with Gusto framework in the next eight chapters.

In Chapter 4, you will learn how to get a strategic investor and that you will need a deep understanding of the value they are able to uniquely and sustainably create. At the same time, you need to be able to demonstrate your value to them. In Chapter 5, you will learn what kind of investor and investment is the right fit for you. Investors can be a form of outsourcing, and strategic investors come with a knowledge base in their respective fields of expertise.

In Chapter 6, you will learn how to streamline your customer channels, so you are clear and efficient. Your voice will become relevant to those you speak to; you will want them to listen and know more about your value proposition. These three steps dovetail together as the foundation of the framework. I've separated them out here, but they really work together. In order to find the right investor, you need to know what value you bring to the table, and you need to know how to find customers. That's the Venn diagram you need to start your strategic money search.

In Chapter 7, you will learn how to be a great customer to your suppliers and why it matters. Transactional relationship with suppliers is one-dimensional. All you are offering them is money in exchange for their product. Sell an added value back to them, and the transaction now becomes mutually beneficial. In Chapter 8, you will learn where you need to focus the most time and what is most important to your business' success. You only have twenty-four hours in a day, so make them count. Give yourself a virtual rate per hour and see where in your business it is most needed. In Chapter 9, you will learn how to evaluate if you are creating the value they believed you could and how to improve that value creation systematically and strategically.

These three chapters fit together to help you understand at a deeper level what an investor is looking for. They want a partner who can demonstrate not just a good idea and a customer channel but a certain level of business sophistication.

In Chapter 10, you will learn when to hold 'em, know when to fold 'em, when to walk away and when to run. Every business goes through cycles. Your business model should be fluent, but you only need to adapt when the time is right. In Chapter 11, you will come to understand your life is business and you are the actual product. You sell yourself to all those around you every day, so know what you are selling of yourself and how to increase that self-value offer.

In Chapter 12, we will look at how to avoid self-sabotage and the worst of the mistakes entrepreneurs often make. To avoid falling off a cliff, you first need to see it and know it is there. The final three chapters are the most important in some ways. These chapters speak to the person you are, which, ultimately, is what an investor is putting their money behind. Investors know things will go wrong, so before they give you their money, they want to know that you are the right jockey to bet on for when that happens. Are you ready?

The last philosophy I want to share before we dive into the 7 principles is: "We are the sum total of the choices we make."

Every single day we make different choices. Decisions are compound. One thing I learnt as a rugby player and athlete is that if you work out and eat healthy every day, you will play differently. I might not want to train today, but if I skip it today, I have a reason to skip tomorrow. If I keep making the decision to train, even on the days I don't want, those small choices add up, and on the sporting field, it means you get played more, and get more game time. This is true in business too. You can't keep putting off these tasks I am about to share and expect a good result. The result will come from consistent effort.

So, let's get started and dive into the Build a Business with Gusto framework.

4

KNOW YOUR VALUE

One thing I learnt early on in life is that no time is ever wasted when spent educating yourself or spent gathering information from peers, mentors, and even your family. Studying business does not always make you a professor, and you won't always know things by heart, but it does help you identify familiar aspects of business. I think today, the most important thing I have learnt is that if you do not know something, go read about it.

When I started my journey in the biggest independent supermarket retail group in South Australia, I looked at the business from an investor's perspective. The investors at this point in time were the multi-store operators, and business was always conducted to create as much value for them through the support and investment from the suppliers who supplied these stores. Before I could even try to extract more value from the suppliers, I had to understand the current value-creation process: why are suppliers partnering with the biggest independent supermarket retail group? Why is it that when they have multiple avenues to get their products to the end consumer, they still want to do business and invest with us?

During my first few months, my focus was learning as much of the business as possible. With my exposure to business studies and past working experience, I subconsciously started to notice small details that normally would only come to light if you do a business plan. As I saw these opportunities, I would write them down, and I would assess what value they could add to the current value we were creating and would add to the perceived value of the suppliers. I would then have the opportunity to present to the board why I think thought is a great opportunity and why we should implement it.

Most of the time, new concepts would get implemented, not because I spoke from a position of authority but by practically showcasing the potential value extraction.

One of the opportunities that I saw was that traditionally, suppliers are seen as the giver. I understood that suppliers are limited in the data and information they receive from a performance level. Suppliers wanted a partnership and understanding that their focus is not necessarily to grow their sales but to grow the categories they play in. So, we created a partnership program that was focused on this. We measured performance feedback not only on their products but also on their contribution to the categories as a whole and the total growth achieved. We could only have done this by understanding our current position, what the supplier needs are, and what it is we can offer.

The key to securing strategic investors is demonstrating your ability to sustainably create value. Investors aim to reduce uncertainty around projections and returns. The more you can showcase measurable value beyond assumptions, the stronger your pitch.

While passion matters, even the most charming entrepreneurs need substantiated plans. Success stems from understanding your competitive position thoroughly first, not overestimating potential. Let's explore how to convey your value and competitive edge convincingly.

ANALYSE YOUR VALUE PROPOSITION

To move forward, you have to know what your starting position is. Take stock of what you have and understand the market dynamics that will potentially influence your business creation journey. You are the window to your current or potential business investors, who, more often than not, invest because of the individual, not because you are probably a charming, nice person, but because you have shown invested time, knowledge, and understanding of your current or potential business.

You answer these questions by asking questions. There are multiple business frameworks that can be used to help you ask the right questions.

A SWOT (Strengths, Weaknesses, Opportunities, Threats) analysis is a great way to understand your current value proposition, what it could be, or even what it might not be. A SWOT analysis provides a structured way to assess your strengths, weaknesses, opportunities and threats.

Identify strengths setting you apart from competitors. What unique resources or capabilities make you more competitive?

Ask yourself:

- What are the things you are doing well or will be setting you apart from your competitors?
- What are the competitive advantages you will have over others?
- What unique resources will you have that will give you an added advantage?

Next, note weaknesses compromising your performance. What could be improved? Ask yourself:

- What are the things your potential competitors are doing well that are not easy to replicate?
- What type of complaints or whispers that you hear in the market about your industry and business?
- What is it that you can improve?

Pinpoint current or emerging opportunities through market trends or leverage your strengths further. What resources do you lack, or do competitors have an advantage on? Ask yourself:

- What are my current and future potential opportunities?
- What external factors can give us a greater competitive advantage?
- How can we turn our strengths into opportunities?
- What trends can we take advantage of?
- What market opportunities are present that we can take advantage of?

Finally, determine threats from competitors, obstacles needing resolution, and vulnerabilities from weaknesses. Ask yourself:

- What obstacles do we need to overcome?
- What are our competitors doing?
- What threats can hurt our business?
- Are any of our weaknesses exposing us to potential threats?

Creating an honest SWOT assessment illuminates areas for targeted improvement.

For a prospective business, estimate your future value proposition. Research competitors and industry dynamics thoroughly. Collect insights from current pain points and whispers in your market. Understand why current solutions fail to satisfy needs. This intelligence will fuel your competitive plan.

CALCULATE COSTS AND EFFICIENCIES

Investors understand that the financial reward comes from the sustainable value that the business can create. Showcasing this through tangible and sometimes quantifiable means creates measurable assessment of the potential. To do this, you have to rigorously estimate costs across your entire value chain – from raw materials to finished goods or services. Account for all inputs affecting pricing like transportation, storage, human resources, rent, administration, taxes, and equipment. Analyse each input for efficiencies without compromising quality.

I helped one distribution company realise savings by optimising delivery routes and negotiating supplier discounts on high-volume ingredients without changing formulations. Even minor efficiencies add up, expanding profit margin, but we can't find those savings if you don't know the actual cost of your offer.

Here's what a yes looks like – this is where the value is created for investors.

In the simplest form, understanding the true value creation of the business and subtracting the true cost of the business creates the reward. The further you are able to demonstrate the gap between these two, the better you are able to articulate the reward to investors.

You can demonstrate that there are efficiencies in the current cost structure. This can be achieved by demonstrating a way you can get it at the same cost but have efficiencies in the distribution channel or there are efficiencies in sourcing or creating the products or services you intend to supply.

You can also demonstrate that there is a new market to tap into or a current established client base ready for distribution. Both of these can showcase an increase in revenue. Again, the further you are able to demonstrate the gap between revenue and cost, the bigger the reward.

In my experience, investors try to avoid uncertainty. Common mistakes or misconceptions many aspiring entreprencurs make are when there is an overconfidence of the potential performance or a lack of understanding the cost of sale.

Customers will be easy to come by? No, they won't; the success of other companies does not guarantee their customer base will now be yours. Most companies have spent many dollars to capture and retain customers. We can source raw products cheaper than current competitors, but you have not taken into account the full product creation and channel costs involved.

I have been involved with four individuals currently working in the insecticides industry and the first discussion we had was that we can source the product cheaper, and they are going to sell it to these people at volume. But none of this was substantiated. Through a few discussions, we discovered that, but they didn't understand all aspects influencing the value proposition.

We identified that they don't have the intellectual property (IP), and if they did, how long would it be for the next IP?

The main model they were aiming for was cutting out the middleman my question was, "Why didn't they do it themselves?" If we are four guys sitting around a table, why didn't the company do it?

We identified that the product would have the same formulations, so what's the competitive advantage or unique value proposition. If it is just going to do exactly what other products will do why buy ours. As per my normal process I started asking questions, the questions focused first on why they might think other companies have not pursued the same strategy. Questions like:

- Does it take a lot of time and effort to create new products that could scare of other competitors not pursuing the same avenue?
- What legislation requirements are required for these types of products? Is it a hard and tedious process that must be potentially renewed often?
- Is there enough money to make it worth the effort?
- Is there associated risk (a.k.a. with a white label) that scares other competitors enough to avoid going with this strategy?

I followed up with questions that are more focused around their market strategy.

- Are there any intellectual property or call outs that makes you different?

- If we do manage to stand out, what is the strategy to make standing out sustainable?
- Once we have market share and prove the concept, why can't competitors replicate it?

They weren't able to answer those as what they saw was that they could source a product cheaper, so they had to be able to sell more.

The most compelling demonstrations showcase durable competitive advantages that are difficult for others to replicate or circumvent. This protects your value proposition over time.

For example, patented technology that enhances capabilities and cannot be easily copied without infringing provides a legal advantage. Brand reputation and customer loyalty also foster stickiness that competitors struggle to overcome. Analyse whether any of your strengths or capabilities have these sustainable barriers to imitation or substitution.

UNCOVER SUSTAINABLE ADVANTAGES

When I started the Seasons Supermarket group in Queensland, I identified that there was an opportunity for high-end quality supermarkets with a great shopping experience. We were not focused on turnover but understood that we could make more margins when the quality and experience is not questioned. Traditional supermarkets don't think this way – it's hard to focus on value and experience – big retail is all about cost … *it's easier to run a business based on price.*

You can just look at supermarket advertising, and it's mostly about price and why they are the cheapest. This can only be achieved through reducing your cost structure, and you can't create quality and experience and have a low-cost structure altogether.

All the stores bought in Queensland had the traditional mindset; we renovated and changed the product offer in every store, and after twelve months, we nearly doubled the profits with increased sales while demanding a higher margin. Why? Because we identified a shopper who was willing to pay for the experience and go home with gourmet products they could not get in other stores focused on price.

Your job is to know the difference between your actual value and competitive advantage and your imagined best-case scenario. An idea is only as strong as the business model, execution plan, and defensible advantages backing it up.

Demonstrating your thorough understanding of these key drivers provides a roadmap even in uncertain terrain. In the coming chapters, we will be building that road map together, but before we get to that, we have to understand what kind of investors are right for you because the map is different if the location we are driving to is different. With compelling substantiation, investors can clearly evaluate the opportunity and projected returns and determine if it's right for them. You need to be able to understand if it's right for you.

5

YOUR KIND OF INVESTOR

Kombucha is a growing trend for health-conscious consumers and one of the fastest-growing categories in beverages. I worked with a small company that identified this trend and created a range of products with a unique value proposition with their uniquely grown personal recipes. They also used local provinces for support and product differentiation.

From a product and value perspective, it was great. Sales were increasing, and the customer base was growing. After four years, the business had not made much money yet, and with limited cash flow, they could not promote growth, and sustainability became a question mark. They knew that they would need a cash injection if they wanted to take the business to a new level. I started working with them and soon realised that it was not just cashflow they needed, but they also needed structure and basic business principles implementation. They had never explored efficiencies in the way they produced their products; they had no understanding of their current stock count or wastage and did not even have any form of meetings among themselves discussing key performance indicators.

They only focused on making a product at a perceived cost and selling it at a perceived value but could not understand why they were not making money. So, the answer for them was more cash flow to make more stock and sell more. Working with them, we outlined these principles, and at the top of the list was a skill set that created the structure the company desperately needed. They approached a potential investor and were willing to forgo 25 percent shareholding for $25k. Now, in the grand scheme of things, $25k is not a lot for 25 percent shares, but the reality is that the books did not show profits matching up to valuing their business at $25k.

At their introduction and on my advice, they requested that the investor had to commit time to the business as well. The need for structure would have been fully satisfied by this investor. Now, the investor did not mind paying $25K, but your company, on paper, is technically broke. However, the investor saw the potential and offered $10k as goodwill, his time to create structure and processes in the business, as well as a loan amount to fund the cash flow needs for future growth. All returns the investor would have received would have been a direct result of the growth of the company, no salaries, just growth. The company was so fixated on getting in the $25k because they wanted some reward for the four years they worked so hard and did not put a value on the knowledge and experience the investor offered. They ended up creating a GoFundMe portal selling to 500 shareholders and raised a $105k – job "well done." Six months later, the cash had been absorbed, and they are back at square one.

THE POWER OF STRATEGIC INVESTORS

Strategic investors provide capital plus hands-on mentorship to accelerate growth. They take an active role guiding major decisions and providing expertise to amplify the capabilities of your existing team. A strategic investor creates accountability leads to stability and sustainability. It can also give you the time to focus on the things that you are good at, the things that have brought you to where you are at that point in time. Strategic investors also leverage existing networks. Early Snapchat investor Lightspeed Venture Partners introduced founders to Facebook later on, leading to lucrative partnerships. Determining where your team could benefit from supplemental experience allows you to vet investor fit beyond just capital amounts. Now, an investor, by its nature, is about the return. On one spectrum, some investors want to be silent partners; they want a concrete, low-risk investment with no involvement except for getting feedback on how the company is performing. Banks and loans will also fall under this banner, as you will know the expected loan amount and expected cost of returns. On the other spectrum, you have strategic investors who love to help create new businesses and be part of the journey. This gives them a sense of ownership and control of their investment.

Many entrepreneurs can look past the arrogance of believing they can do without any assistance and understand the value a strategic investor can bring. Strategic investors' knowledge base is usually across multiple sectors, but they report to tried and tested business foundations that work for them. It's even better if you have a strategic investor who has knowledge and leverage in the industry you will be entering. They can create economies of scale or even break down barriers to entry. Now, the silent partner can only offer you one thing, and that is money, whereas the strategic investor can give you money, their time, and their knowledge. There is no right or wrong investor, and it's totally based on what you have identified as the need within your company.

THE APPEAL AND LIMITATIONS OF SILENT INVESTORS

Many entrepreneurs seek silent investors to maximise autonomy. Silent partners provide capital without wanting an active role in operations or decision-making. This allows you to maintain control of your company vision and strategy. Silent investors expect concrete returns based on a low-risk investment thesis without involvement beyond monitoring financial performance. Typical silent funding sources include banks, angel investors, and some private equity firms.

For example, when Uber was still a fledgling startup, it secured early silent funding from First Round Capital and other VC firms who provided capital but not hands-on guidance. The advantage of a silent investor is the autonomy you maintain in your business.

Many entrepreneurs have their business concept 90 percent sorted and identified cash flow as their main and only constraint. They have identified that there is enough skillset in the business to create and execute the value propositions in a structural manner. My experience is that one of the main drivers of becoming an entrepreneur is to be your own boss. It's a hard road to be on, but many find this worth it. Silent investors generally will invest for a set time period and will want an easy exit. By knowing the time expectations investors are looking to invest for, you will know when and how much you have to add to your balance sheet, as this will be a forecasted cost. The longer the term, the more manageable the costs will be.

ASSESSING YOUR CAPITAL AND EXPERTISE NEEDS

The reality is that it's not just about getting money. You want to think about what *kind* of money you want and what time and knowledge you need. Do you just want smart money, strategic advice, or even both? Every business reaches an inflection point where bringing on an investor can provide the fuel for growth or the expertise to get to the next level. But not all investors are created equal. In this chapter, we will compare silent investors who provide just capital versus strategic investors who also contribute hands-on guidance. Consider your end goals and current skills gaps to determine if you need capital alone or capital plus strategic guidance:

- If you seek greater control and have strong confidence in your existing team, a silent cash infusion may suffice.
- If you want to accelerate growth through expertise and access outside your network, a strategic investor may be preferable.

A STRATEGIC PARTNERSHIP CASE STUDY

Just as I was finishing up this chapter, I received a call from Adam, an irrigation expert who was running a sole trader's company servicing and installing irrigation systems. He identified a need to open up an irrigation supply store in a growing town with booming development. His idea was to integrate into the supply chain, get irrigation items at resale cost, and sell it to customers while still doing his normal work. He wanted efficiency all the way through the supply chain that he could take advantage of. He had this great idea, and his knowledge base of irrigation can never be questioned, but he was overwhelmed with the idea of setting up a new business and did not know where to start. I agreed to work with him on the project to help create direction and a framework for his new venture.

Together, we created the store concept and had a full

business plan ready for execution, but we had to find the right premises at the right cost to create a sustainable business. Time passed, and finding an ideal location proved to be difficult, and he quickly got discouraged. As mentioned, part of his reason was that he would still grow the irrigation business but supply himself through the store. Because we articulated the business plan and identified future potential opportunities, we identified that focusing on landscaping and a total water solution, domestic and commercial, would widen his current business offering.

His need for a strategic partner had more value than money on the table. He now shares a 50-percent ownership with a strategic partner who is time-invested in the business. Adam is the face of the business, but his partner (strategic investor) has laid down the structure, business model and needed cash flow for the business. In six months, the newly founded company already made the same turnover Adam made in twelve months on his own. Adam forfeited 50 percent of his business for $0 in exchange for the strategic investor's knowledge, time, and cash flow. They identified that finding the right location is still cumbersome, so to break this barrier, they created a virtual online store; they managed to get listed as a preferred reseller by suppliers and now enjoy the economies of scale in the reduction of product supply costs. Two similar stories with similar needs, two different outcomes.

6

THE CUSTOMER IS KING

A value proposition is exactly what it means – an identified consumer need that you specifically designed, created a value for, and offered to customers. To create a clear and sustainable value proposition, your business model and all the moving parts within are created and focused to maximise the creation and the delivery of value. A value proposition also becomes the foundation of your decision-making when creating products and services, and everything you do should always end up with your value proposition in mind.

When you try to be everything for everyone, the value creation process becomes foggy and unclear. What value am I focusing on today? What customer am I targeting? Is the key performance task set out for the day focused on today's value proposition or the next one? There are various forces in every market that sometimes will bend, stretch, and question the value proposition you currently have and sometimes thinking, "let me cover all my bases," will eliminate this, but the reality is that the narrower your value offer is, the better you will understand how it is created and identify the forces influencing it. The 3M company is particularly good in understanding that they do not sell sticky notes or paper; their core business is the quality of its adhesive, the glue that makes things stick.

ALIGNING VALUE PROPOSITIONS WITH TARGET MARKETS

Within the supermarket industry, there has been an evolution from just selling dry goods and basic needs products to offering on-the-go food solutions, warm hot meals, freshly cut meat, and even coffee. So, by widening the customer needs target, you can capture more sales, right? Well, not if it is not part of your core value proposition. If your value proposition is just price-focused, you will have to sell the new added value at a discounted price. A price-driven model will only work when it's accommodated by a low-cost structure; remember, the wider the gap between volume and cost, the bigger the reward. Supermarkets that have adopted a value-driven rather than volume-driven model will have better success in executing this type of strategy as they know who their target customers are, and they know they shop there for value and quality and are willing to pay the price.

On one of my business trips, I had this craving for a nice curry dish. Not really knowing the area, I naturally searched for the closest place that sold curry dishes. Indian restaurants are world-renowned for their curry, so when I found an Indian restaurant, I was overjoyed. I could not wait to look at the menu and pick my meal. On my arrival, and to my surprise, there were only two curry options, neither of which was particularly appealing in light of the fact I could also get burgers, sushi, pizza. and even ice cream. This was a great example of a restaurant that was trying to make meals for everyone. First, they confuse the consumer by calling themselves an Indian restaurant but not creating the value that meets the expectations. There was nothing that really set them apart from any competing restaurants. Their clients will be easily interchangeable, and creating loyalty and rapport with the customer through marketing means is even more difficult.

It's harder to create a business model when you create it for an expected target market rather than a target market that is in need of the value proposition you have set yourself up to create. The value proposition and customer target markets should always reinforce each other. Your value will fill your target market's needs, your target market will give you feedback on what can be better or what they love, and then you can tweak your offer to further strengthen your value proposition, building even more loyalty and rapport.

Being able to demonstrate that you have an understanding and focused target market creates credibility with potential investors. As you know by now, the notion "it will be easy to get customers" is not true and showing that you intend to be focused helps articulate and communicate a strategy that will make sense to an investor.

When we created a supermarket offer that focused on quality, great shopping experience, and entertainment, we used these value propositions as the foundation of our target market. We understood that our most likely target market would be your middle to upper-class consumer who has a higher disposable income. Price was not their only decision-making criteria. They would rather pay a dollar extra for a banana that they can take home and still eat seven days later instead of having to throw it away the next day because it is over-ripe. We did not make more money on that extra dollar because we paid extra for that banana, but we communicated effectively about where we source the product from and why it is worth the extra dollar.

We understood that these consumers are more digital-savvy, and social media platforms play a big part in their daily lives. We managed to create an opt-in loyalty email program for these customers, sending out, on average, 30,000 emails a week with an open rate of 37 percent, which is good by any standards.

Our message was always clear, "Sustainable quality with a touch of difference." We knew our strong suit was gourmet products and products you would not find in your traditional supermarket retailers. So instead of just focusing on everyday known items, we would advertise our gourmet sauces, our olive oil that contains twenty-four-carat gold flakes, or some of our 500 different selections of cheese.

We also understood that the target customer was very community-focused. Our first choice of supplier would always be someone local, but only if they are able to add to our value proposition of sustainable quality. We supported local welfare organisations and had a big focus on youth development in our direct surrounding community.

IMITATION WITHOUT INSIGHT BACKFIRES

A common mistake that companies make is to copycat other businesses. Now I'm all for learning what competitors are doing, but you should just eat the meat and spit out the bones. If they have done it right, they will be able to back what they are offering and communicating; they have had time to perfect their products and offer and by following them you will always be a step behind with a lack of understanding why and how they are doing it in the first place.

It is human nature to follow success, thinking, "if someone else can do it, I can too, right?"

In landscaping, some of the companies drill water holes, so because Adam's business is now a full water solutions business it should only be natural to do the same. Some might see an opportunity, think "we could do that," but don't really understand everything that needs to be done. Firstly, obtaining a drilling machine from a financial standpoint is vastly different to some water pipes installed in a front yard. Adam has never drilled holes before, and the added responsibility could make him lose the focus on what is currently being sought from him and his strategic investor.

A renowned publishing company had a dry run and looked at avenues that could supplement their income. Now another trend is selling Facebook ads within their industry, so if others can do it, why can't they? So, they started selling Facebook ads to bridge a financial gap and they thought, "easy money! We don't need a loan." But without the clear processes and the clear value or USP, they ended up moving team members over to focus on this new revenue stream; as a result, their core and current value proposition was not getting the love it needed and their old product broke, clients got upset, and the lost revenue and bad will created was more damaging than the initial dry run they experienced. It actually cost them more than they made even though they could sell services and books.

SHOWCASING VALUE AND STRATEGY SECURES INVESTMENT

Why was the strategic investor willing to invest time, knowledge, and money in a canning company that was technically broke regardless that the company chose a different route? Why was Adam able to get an investor in a landscaping business that hit a growth ceiling? Well, in both instances, they were able to demonstrate two key aspects for investors. One, they were able to demonstrate a good understanding of the value they created and who their target segment was. Secondly and most importantly, they were able to demonstrate that the injection of cash flow was not to keep the current company afloat. They were able to showcase what the money would have been spent on to create additional value for their target markets and a focused strategy on how to get the product to the customer.

7

BEING A GREAT CUSTOMER

By now, we all know that maximising revenue and lowering the cost of delivering value creates the reward. This is the foundation of business success and, if done well, will create sustainability and longevity in your business. So, if this is true for you as an entrepreneur, why wouldn't it be true for your suppliers, as well?

Suppliers create their model in the same manner and need to extract as much value from executing their value proposition as you do. In life, I believe that if you help others to get what they want, you will get what you want.

THE SUPPLIER PARTNERSHIP MINDSET

Playing in multiple team sports and learning that I'm part of a whole really resonated with me in business as well as my personal life. As a rugby player, I relied on my teammates to execute plays together. If I didn't practice passing drills with my number nine, we would fumble hand-offs. If I didn't coordinate with flankers on timing, our runs would fail. The same went for cricket. My bowling success depended on fielders catching any nicks. As a bowler, I needed my wicketkeeper to be in sync on catches. Practising together and keeping a team mindset were key to bettering my personal performance.

This same team concept applies to suppliers. When you create your value proposition, you have two spectrums of focus. On the one side, you create the value, and on the other, you execute it. Suppliers have multiple avenues to deliver their products or services to the end consumer, so why work with you?

UNDERSTANDING SUPPLIER GOALS

Take time to understand your supplier's model and help *them* make money, and *you* will make money. Help them build rapport with the customers, and you will build rapport with the customers, too.

Some companies, unfortunately, take an adversarial stance with their suppliers, dictating terms and demanding concessions. This may work in the short-term but often backfires. I've seen businesses squeeze suppliers upfront only to lose access to key materials and damage those relationships long-term. For example, a former employer demanded 30 percent lower prices from their key supplier. They threatened to drop the supplier if they didn't comply. The supplier relented, but quality suffered, and delays increased.

Within a year, the supplier cut ties and signed an exclusive deal with our competitor, leaving us scrambling. Approaching suppliers with threats rather than collaboration hurts in the end.

Too often, businesses demand value from suppliers because we are paying them, right? Yes, you are, but are they making money for you as well?

In contrast, I've seen the power of true supplier partnerships. When you want your supplier to make money and help them build their brand, become their favourite family member.

A client of mine made a point to understand their produce supplier's business model and challenges. They helped the supplier promote their sustainable farming practices on packaging and in joint marketing materials. This built immense trust and goodwill. When an equipment failure jeopardised an order, the supplier went above and beyond to deliver on time – something they admitted likely wouldn't do for other customers. They became not just a vendor but a core partner in delivering an exceptional product.

COLLABORATION FOR MUTUAL BENEFIT

My experience in dealing with suppliers has always started with focusing on what would make them use my channel rather than others. When I started building a relationship program with suppliers, it was their program, not mine. The key performance items would always be focused on their key performance areas. I would first start off with understanding what their current market share is, then set a goal of what market share they want to be. I will then measure this against their share of my business and see if it correlates with the industry norm and then set my goals. We would then go into sub-categories and measure them in the same manner and then do the same by product.

Once I understood what their goals were, I would ask the question of what their focused products are. What products do they really make money from? Most suppliers will get their 80 percent volume of sales from only 20 percent of their products on offer. And for most suppliers to maintain volume, you have to be market competitive so effectively it leaves 20 percent to really make money from. Putting an action plan in place to grow this 20 percent for suppliers shows suppliers' mutual intent and compassion.

Here are some keys to being a great partner to your suppliers:

- Seek to understand their goals and help them achieve success. If their ship rises, so does yours.
- Promote their brand and value proposition to your shared customers when appropriate.
- Collaborate on co-marketing campaigns and events to maximise reach.
- Share data and insights to help suppliers improve targeting and performance.
- Negotiate terms fairly and creatively to benefit both parties on pricing and payment terms.

CREATIVE WIN-WIN NEGOTIATION

As you know, cash flow is just as important to suppliers as it is for you; there's value to be extracted in discussing payment terms with suppliers. In business, we get taught that the best business is to extend your creditors and get into debtors as soon as possible. Though this is true, it is also true for suppliers. If your cash flow allows you to help suppliers on the same basis, why would they not extend value back to you?

Creative payment terms can be a win-win for supplier relationships. A previous employer faced a major cash crunch, but suppliers were extremely flexible in providing extended payment plans without reducing shipments. The owner was transparent about the situation, and each supplier negotiated tailored terms to keep the product flowing. In the end, all parties were made whole. That good faith and trust preserved a thriving business. When cash gets tight, view payment negotiations through a partnership lens.

Part of the success we achieved in our retail business was our fresh produce offering. The quality was supreme; our apples were flawless and shiny, our bananas lasted for multiple days, and our grapes were juicy and sweet. And part of this success was that 80 percent of our produce we received from one supplier. We understood that their model was aligned with ours. Their supply chain allowed their fresh produce to be sourced from selected farmers and kept under temperature control from the farm all the way to our display cabinets. We understood that we couldn't pay the same price for their products in comparison to other providers. We understood that we had to build their relationship with the customers to give them more value than a paycheck. Together, we created a marketing campaign that educated the consumers about their business and soon started creating their brand in the marketplace. The rapport we managed to build and the success of the growth in fresh produce led to other retailers wanting the same and led to new business. We helped them to get what they wanted, so we got what we wanted.

NAVIGATING THE UNEVEN PLAYING FIELD

A lot of companies try to dictate, and they can. The bitter *and* sweet of retail lies within the volume a channel can provide for suppliers. Major retailers have such a big footprint that suppliers will bend over backwards just to get a piece of this volume. They have to pay listing fees, have to pay rebates on sales done, have to pay for marketing campaigns, and even have to pay for supporting new product development and launches. If suppliers choose not to participate, the majors will just shrug their shoulders and say good luck to you. Now, I can't say that this is true for all major companies, and I'm sure there are those who have a relationship mindset, but I have yet to find an industry where this is not the case.

Smaller retailers do not have this luxury, so what do you do? Well, you help the suppliers make money. You help them by being able to extract more value from the

20 percent of sales so that you can extract more value out of your sales. I believe in value-driven businesses and not volume. Sometimes, you can do less turnover and still make the same money as you would have made chasing volume.

For most businesses, it's not easy to create the same relationship with all suppliers. Retail stores can do business with up to 400 suppliers, and it is physically impossible to give the same attention to all. This does not mean that you can't create a platform that is universal to all, a platform that shows the intent of mutual thinking and goal-setting.

BONDS BUILT IN SUNSHINE SUSTAIN IN STORMS

I have been involved with a distribution company that acted as a buying group for independent retailers. The CEO and founder first worked for a similar company that had the dictating supplier's mindset and also dictated to its independent retailers. He was inspirational and a mentor in the way he thought to create value for suppliers and customers. He, too, realised that if you help the suppliers and customers to get what they want, you will get what you want. He managed to create a business that was value-driven for its suppliers and soon became one of the major independent buying groups in South Africa.

But the journey was not always easy. There was a time when a major independent customer went into forced liquidation, owing this buying group millions of dollars. Needless to say, this created massive cash flow problems, and for all intended purposes, the writing was on the wall. Now, it was at this point the real return came from the suppliers. The relationships that were built with suppliers and the compassion that was created by working on mutual goals created a platform for open and honest communication. Suppliers presented themselves with payment terms that would help the buying group pay off its debt while still maintaining business as usual. Suppliers understood that if they helped this business through this hard time, they would get the return in the future. This held true; all debt was successfully paid, and the business is still yet to have a year where it has not displayed growth for suppliers.

Building strong supplier relationships gives you access to better pricing, products, service, and more. Suppliers are fundamental partners in executing your value proposition. Take time to understand their goals, co-market your brands, collaborate creatively, and approach negotiations fairly. When you help suppliers achieve success, they will return the favour in spades. Treat suppliers like the teammates they are.

8

KEY ACTIVITIES

Setting up a business – a.k.a. the growing phase of any business – is a daunting task. The call to create a new business or grow your business is powerful, but where do you begin? Why do people struggle to see a dream in reality? Dreams are in concept, don't have time, have no real beginning or end, and are foggy – the same as a vision. This is daunting, but mapping it out makes it real and tangible, and when you're visually able to see the dream become a reality, you will find your footing.

A business model is a snapshot in time of the current influences that help you create the value proposition and deliver it to the customers. But business models are also fluent; we make many decisions in business that can change the way we do business. Changing one part of the business has a ripple effect on the different aspects of the creation and delivery spectrum. When we bought over existing supermarkets, their model was based on product and price. Now, we already decided that we wanted to be a value-driven business focused on delivering quality sustainable products through great service and shopping experience. So, our value proposition was different to the current offer and, inherently, the current model had to adapt. The store already had an established client base used to the current offer, so what effect would it have on them, what potential new customers could we attract, and what product offers needed to change?

LAYING THE GAME PLAN

In rugby, every move starts with a well-rehearsed set play. Similarly, in business, your value proposition is that game plan. Just as a fly-half wouldn't kick without a purpose, every business decision should align with your core value. Think of your business model as your team lineup – it's fluid, adaptable, and every player (or aspect of your business) has a role to play. Just as a cricket team might adjust their fielding positions based on the batsman, your business might need to tweak its strategy based on the competition and market environment.

Staying true to your value proposition sets the tone for decision-making. Every decision made has this in mind, from sourcing and building relationships, to selling and communicating our offer to the customers. Building and documenting your model helps you see how all the parts make a whole and how they interact with each other. You have to identify the key activities that influence your value proposition. You have to tie your value proposition to your customers and suppliers and assign critical, moderate, or low classifications to them; don't launch anything critical without a system and key performance activities in place.

Creating your value proposition is at the heart of your model. But do not keep this a secret. Your value proposition is only as good as the people living it around you. Training, communicating, and creating a value proposition-focused culture is of utmost importance to any business. Your peers, staff, and even suppliers need to be on board for it to truly come to reality.

So, what factors will create a value-driven model for us? We understood that our focus points were "quality," "customer service," and "shopping experience." The quality of produce was set to a new standard, only A-grade products were allowed, and quality control checks were put in place to make sure this standard was maintained. We increased our product range with a wider selection of gourmet products from gourmet sources to a big range of cheese from around the world. We did the same quality process within our butchery department and changed the size and quality of our hot foods offered. We wanted to create a different customer experience, and the most direct impact we could make was the look and feel of the business. We installed wooden flooring throughout the whole business and installed delicatessen display cabinets with greenery on display everywhere you looked. Customers would want to stay and wonder and should not feel that shopping was a task.

Once the value proposition is segmented, you can

understand how to create and deliver it. Focus on the key activities you have set out to make this happen.

Identify the individuals or groups that your business is trying to target with your product. Creating segments based on demographics can help you identify the key differences between each group and how you can better serve each. We did not buy any store that became available. We knew we wanted customers with more disposable income, so we selected areas that brought us closer to them. We understood the demographics of the neighbourhood, what country they originated from, their median age, how many households and occupants were living in it, and we even knew how many households had pets and what kind of pets they were. National surveys can give you a wealth of information and are mostly easily accessible. Because part of our value proposition was being community-focused, we could make the decision if we wanted to keep country-specific products to resonate with different demographics and use this as a means of building relationships with customers.

We had to understand the needs of the local community; maybe a low-cost model was the correct one, but by studying available income compared to the local share of the market, we concluded that money on retail was spent outside of the local community, so could this be a value-driven need for customers getting fulfilled somewhere else?

Understanding your customer segment can also establish the size of your potential market. This will influence how you communicate with them and the channels of distribution. Traditionally, a low-cost model is associated with mass marketing. Value-driven models traditionally have a niche market, so the channels of communication are more directed and more personal.

There are ways in which your business will deliver and communicate with your customers. Channels are the ways in which you can raise awareness for your business and product. Remember that channels can also come through your key partners! Opting for a value-driven communication channel, social media became a strong focus. You can be more targeted in where you want to deliver your offer. Loyalty card implementation also brought us closer to the customer; customers could choose to receive communication or not, so the ones who did had a higher probability of looking at what you had to offer. Partnering with local communities and events creates a sense of commitment to the community. Customers see this as an emotional investment in them and strengthen brand recognition.

It's also important to note that marketing is one of those costs that is not always directly measurable. It's almost like changing your car tires. You know it makes the car safer to drive, but how do you measure it until you don't change your car tires at all and see what happens? We tried various techniques to see the impact of marketing. When doing community events, we monitored community pages to see if there was any mention of our brand. When promoting specific products, we monitored the potential uplift in sales not only at that point in time but even when it was not on promotion, asking the question, "Did we manage to increase the average daily sales over time?"

You have to build a relationship with your customers. Identify each of your customer segments and list out the relationship your business has with that individual group. Include details about how your business interacts with them, how interactions might be different amongst customers, how you are maintaining customer relationships, and how your business can continue to grow its customer base. We used in-store product education as a means of building this relationship and trust. Informing customers about what you have to offer shows that you care about their needs and why you think they will be satisfied with your offer. This can also be achieved with personalisation through email marketing platforms; today, you can send mass emails that address the person personally at the introduction and make the customer feel that it was sent only to them. Personal service and interaction normally take place within the customers' personal space; they can either close up and not accept you or let you in. Having a gusto attitude is contagious, and customers are more likely to let you in.

Your revenue stream is mainly a result of creating your value proposition, communicating it to the target market, and then accepting it and making the purchase. Understanding how you generate the revenue helps you focus on what influences it. You need to understand what strategies you can employ to capture the most value from your customers. Having a value-driven model does not mean you can request the highest possible price for your offer. What are customers willing to pay for the perceived value that they are not getting from your competitors?

Product and price are not the only means of revenue. By giving suppliers what they want, you will get what you want. In other words, if you create additional tangible value to suppliers, they will be willing to reward you for it. Marketing does not just have to be a cost centre but can be turned into a profit centre. Suppliers generally will pay money to have their products advertised to the target market. Many suppliers allow for a rebate relationship in return for continued support and representation in your business. When you change your mindset of making the supplier your customer as well, you can identify all the sellable key activities you have established in your model and market it to your new customer: your supplier.

To create a value proposition, you need to understand what significant resources your value proposition requires. Which significant resources do our distribution channels require? What significant resources do our customer relationships require? Which significant resources do our revenue streams require? There are various types of resources you will need to answer all these questions. Financial resources are the bloodline of the business. Understanding your cash flow needs and where it's coming from allows you to maximise sustainability and manage growth. Human resources are an extension of yourself. They allow you to do things you cannot do or do not have the time to do. They can bring a wealth of knowledge, but you need to know what knowledge you need for your business and value proposition. You don't need an accountant to price items, but you might need an accountant for book-keeping if you can't manage it yourself.

Key partners are the external suppliers or companies that will help you deliver your value proposition to your customers. Be sure to include the value these partners provide to your business. You need to know who these partners are and what role they will play within your value creation.

One of the most overlooked and misunderstood activities I find with entrepreneurs, and what's also very important for potential investors, is your understanding and ability to identify all the key costs associated with operating your business model and delivering on your value proposition to your customers. You have to understand the major costs incurred by your business and which sectors of your business require funding in order for your business to run smoothly. Costings can be managed by knowing what primary resources and activities are the most expensive; can this be substituted or outsourced?

NAVIGATING THE FIELD

Imagine your target market as the opposing rugby team. If you've studied their moves (or, in business terms, their buying habits), you'll be better positioned to intercept their passes and score tries. And just as a cricket team uses stats to strategise against opponents, businesses should use market data to tailor their approach.

For example, if your store is in a neighbourhood with many expats from a rugby-loving nation, perhaps hosting game day specials or themed events might be a winning strategy. If a particular product isn't "scoring" with your customers, it's time to change the play – just as a cricket captain might bring on a spinner instead of a fast bowler when conditions change.

It's easy to get confused about what comes now and what comes later. Creating a road map so you understand what you need to do now (because it's critical to your value creation) and what you can do when you hit certain milestones. Labour is a big part of our cost structure but still remains critical to the success of our business. Within retail, we looked at the key activities the human resources perform and what could be changed or become more efficient. Every week we had a set of new special pricing, and we had to change pricing tickets on the shelf to advertise. This took a considerable amount of labour time and was non-productive. So how did we fix this? Well, we automated it. We installed electronic ticketing systems that could change with the push of a button. What would have taken hours to do from multiple staff members can now be done in a jiffy. It was a big capital expense initially, but for the next ten years, we will save, on average, $57k a year in labour hours. Now we have the choice to either distribute these hours to a key activity that is focused on value-driven items that will generate additional income, or we can bank the savings. The fact that we took the time to understand allowed us to save. Now why did we not do this from the beginning if there were huge savings? It could have been fun to do at the beginning, but if we didn't hit a certain revenue goal to allow these updates, it wouldn't have made sense to do.

As the captain of your team, you need someone to check that you aren't prioritising the projects you think are the most fun as opposed to the activities that create the most value. If you're focused on low cost, you need strong buyers, and if you are focused on value creation, you need design and research. Having an external eye, someone who does not spend day in and day out in your shoes, can help you identify what the key performance indicators (KPIs) within the business are, and this is the reason you don't just want to make money – this is where a strategic advisor / investor can help you identify if you are tracking the right things.

Most investors will also be focused on the mundane tasks but will be critical to understanding your business. They can focus on creating an organisation chart that is going to create the most value and create problem-solving activities. They can also investigate processes and systems conducive to tracking performances through manual or software programs to finance and reporting. Having the right systems to make the right activities streamlined is generally universal and not always industry-specific. Surround yourself with influential individuals and know how they can contribute to your value creation and create accountability.

POST-GAME ANALYSIS

Every rugby team watches replays of their matches, analysing strengths and identifying areas for improvement. Similarly, businesses must review their performance.

Earlier in this book, I spoke about the canning company that I have been involved in. They understood their customers' needs and knew they had a market for canned spring water still and with CO2. But what they did not understand was the real cost of making the product. They never factored in the manual labour cost they used to make the products themselves, how much wastage there was, or how much stock was given away as samples. It was a simple measurement of raw material cost compared to revenue, and in the middle was the thinkable reward but not the real reward. By doing an activity-based cost process, they soon realised that as a business owner, they were actually very expensive canning staff. Now they had tangible information to make economic decisions. They could now evaluate what the cost would be if they employed a junior person to do the canning process and what potential value their free time could add to the business. They could also articulate using a third-party company that could do the canning on their behalf. By knowing the unknown, they were able to make strategic decisions that released value for themselves and for the bottom line.

Like a team realising their best player was in the wrong position, recognising and rectifying missteps in your business approach can be transformative.

9

LEVERAGING COST ANALYSIS TO SECURE CRITICAL INVESTMENT

I had a meeting with four enthusiastic individuals who worked at the same chemical company. They were looking for a strategic investor who could help them initially construct a business model and plan and do a financial investment for 20 percent of the business.

The business was easy. They figured that they could import insecticide chemicals in bulk from international suppliers and land it at the same price on shore as their current company was doing. They already had farmers ready to buy through relationships for the bulk product and would then create their own product brand that we could sell to distribution companies. The focus would be volume-driven, and the profit margin would be circa 200 percent. Now, my knowledge about chemicals is limited, but I do know that making a 200-percent margin in any channel of the retail market is unheard of, and if that is the case, sign me up.

As a strategic investor, you will want to have a firm grasp of the real cost of creating the value throughout the whole value chain. You want to create a system for evaluating on a regular basis if you create your product at the cheapest rate in accordance with your product placement in the market. A natural process of trying to understand a new business and its cost structure is to ask basic questions. These questions should address all key activities focused on creating and executing the value proposition.

As an entrepreneur ready to scale your promising business, undertaking rigorous cost structure analysis is a pivotal step on the path to securing major outside investment. You gain the evidence and projections needed to craft a compelling funding pitch by thoroughly evaluating your cost drivers.

In this chapter, we'll explore how to optimise your cost structures to:

- Demonstrate the viability and profitability of your business model to potential investors.
- Project growth scenarios and returns with credibility to improve investment terms.
- Establish business acumen that gives investors confidence in leadership capabilities.

With detailed cost insights, you can persuasively address the questions prudent investors will ask to minimise their perceived risk. This establishes trust in you as an investment-worthy entrepreneur. Let's dive into the process.

ANALYSING FIXED VS. VARIABLE COSTS

There are two sides of cost structure. On one side, you will want to know the cost of creating the value proposition; on the other, you will want to know the cost of executing it. So, you might think I can buy a widget for $1, modify it for $1, and sell it for $10, but you aren't making $8. To fully price a product, you have to think about staffing, building systems, software, tracking, warehousing, logistics, fuel, and marketing costs. You can't just take the cost of the goods and double or triple it to create maximum efficiency. You have to know what goes into the full cost at the unit cost level to find the levers you can pull.

When assessing the cost to create the value, you will focus on the key activities involved in the business model you created. Cost normally associated with this will be either fixed variable and once off and will be focused on the relationship with your key suppliers, the key activities needed to create the product and your cost structure.

We have already established that suppliers have multiple avenues to get their products in front of the end consumer. Your relationship with these suppliers, whether it's new or historical, is influenced by underlying factors. It so happened that the chemical company the four were working for had a long-standing relationship with the suppliers and, through the years, had built up substantial economies of scale through volume purchases. Even though they worked for the company, it did not give them automatic relationship status. The cost of the product was volume-based, so if you could buy a large amount of volume, you would get the price associated with that volume. When the four approached the supplier for supply, they were not given the same price as their current company or the same payment terms. So, from step one, there was an increase in the cost of goods and the cost of cash flow.

Selecting the right suppliers is also critical. Dealing with suppliers just because competitors do business with them is not necessarily ideal. They need to be aligned with your value offering. The cheapest is not always the best. You have to evaluate current cost vs. sustainability. In our supermarket stores, we do not buy the cheapest refrigeration on the market. We have partnered with a company for a number of years because their products are self-contained and almost 65 percent more energy efficient. They also have prolonged servicing schedules, meaning the amount of time they need to be serviced in a financial year is half the norm. So, we pay upfront for the future savings and can show significant savings on your balance sheet, widening the reward gap between cost and revenue.

Are there alternatives to the products or suppliers that you are currently using? If the value offered by suppliers is the same, are you using the right one? Being able to show the reason for choosing a supplier, whether they are the cheapest now or will create value in the future, will create confidence in this cost base.

The model has already identified the key activities needed to create the value proposition. Human resources in many countries are one of the big three cost items and, if not managed and used correctly, can harm your business. You have to be able to understand that you have the right people in the right seats delivering the right activity. If you grasp the costs, you can decide whether you want to insource or outsource activities. Instead of the insecticides being canned, labelled, and distributed, they can be outsourced to a 3PL logistics company rather than owning a warehouse or factory. This also creates more transparency on the creation cost of the products because the four guys will know exactly the cost to add per unit as charged by the outsourced company. You can also decide to bring your finance in-house rather than outsourcing to an accountant.

When meeting with investors, being able to discern your fixed costs from your variable costs is essential. Fixed costs like rent, equipment leases, and salaries remain constant regardless of sales volume. Variable costs like raw materials and per-unit shipping depend directly on production quantity.

You can realistically project profit margins by modelling fixed vs. variable costs at different scales. This allows investors to evaluate growth scenarios and returns on investment. For example, an investor wants to see that you understand how surging demand may impact material costs but not necessarily rent. Distinguishing fixed vs. variable costs is vital homework before these conversations.

OPTIMISING COST OF GOODS SOLD

The other side of costs is when you execute your value proposition. Your model has shown you how to reach the target market, but it does come at a cost. You have to hold stock for customers to choose from, and in a new set-up, business will have a cash flow impact. You only own the product once the supplier has been paid, and there is a cost of finance whether you have given it yourself, loaned from the bank or got it from the strategic investor. You have to communicate your products to customers. Having the right knowledge for internal marketing comes at a cost, and you should associate this cost to marketing. By knowing the real cost, you can decide to use a marketing company or your strategic suppliers to market for you.

The cost of producing your products or delivering your services will be a prime focus area for investors. To convince them your gross margins are sustainable, do a deep dive into all inputs that comprise cost of goods sold (COGS).

Look for supplier efficiencies – could component materials be sourced cost-effectively without losing quality? Are you purchasing at optimal volumes to receive quantity discounts? Analyse manufacturing processes for waste reduction or automation opportunities. The more discipline you have around COGS, the more credible your projected profit margins will be.

You can have two ways of making mistakes here: firstly, you can try to do everything yourself and have high production and staff costs; secondly, you can outsource everything and lose all your margin. How do you find that balance by knowing what cost is associated with every single key activity, helping you to create your value proposition?

Analysing whether to handle key processes internally or externally provides another lever to optimise costs. Outsourcing delivery may sacrifice some margin but radically reduces staffing, facilities, and equipment costs. The trade-offs require careful calculations grounded in real data.

Thoroughly vetting these "make versus buy" decisions demonstrates analytical thinking and again allows you to credibly project margins at scale. Outlining this analysis also conveys your willingness to flex business models to control costs. These problem-solving skills reassure potential investors.

KEEP YOUR BUSINESS MODEL FLUENT

To secure sizable investment, investors need confidence you will maintain cost discipline as the business grows. Share what cost analysis will be regularly undertaken and KPIs monitored. Highlight how schedules, budgets, and agreements with vendors will inject accountability into keeping costs in check.

Business models are portrayed as fixed or a snapshot

in time, but they are actually fluid and changing. The world has seen how a medical event like never before, COVID, to some degree, changed the landscape of how companies do business, and the reason for this is because one element within their business model and cost structure was affected or changed. Staff started working from home, so businesses vacated commercial real estate. With no businesses to rent to, the target market changed; office space became quarantine or vaccination centres or switched from commercial to residential accommodation. Fast food and coffee shops were not seen as essential services, so they had to close, but supermarkets and chemists didn't. Now, developers are reconstructing their buildings to combine smaller cafes and shops with larger open-space rentals for supermarkets and chemists. They went from a high rate per square income to a lower rate per square, but in return, they receive low-risk tenants with longer-term leases, creating sustainable value. The fast food companies that had to close down started online and delivery when they did not before. They have a kitchen but no walk-in customers, so they used a different channel to reach the target market.

Conveying diligent cost management and controls provides reassurance that your projections will be realised even when changes that require fluidity happen. Investors gain trust by seeing systems baked into the operating model.

The ability to rigorously build and analyse your cost structure from the ground up is a centrepiece of convincing investors your business can deliver sustainable profitability.

Undertaking the exercises in this chapter will equip you with the data and mastery to answer tough questions about the viability of your business model. With fact-based data demonstrating achievable margins, you become an investable entrepreneur.

10

WHEN YOU NEED TO PIVOT

It was the first rugby game of the season, and all the players were ready for the kick-off. The preseason preparations were done, and everyone was on board and ready. Coach Nick clearly articulated the game plan, each player understood exactly what to do and how they would win the game. There was great excitement for the first game, especially with the signing of the new star player, Sebastian. He was the star fly-half who jumped the ranks with his exceptional talent that he time and time again put on display.

Coach Nick had to fight off formidable teams who all wanted this talent, but he knew if they stood any chance this season, Sebastian had to be on his side of the field. The whole game plan was built around Sebastian. The forwards knew they needed to protect the ball and protect Sebastian. The scrum-half knew that he was not allowed to kick the ball but distribute it to Sebastian so that he could work his magic. The whistle blew, and the game was on. Five minutes into the game and,

Sebastian struck; Coach Nick was overjoyed. His game plan was working, and his star recruit was not disappointing. It was almost halftime, and Coach Nick's team led by twenty points. Coach Nick turned to his staff members to show them the thumbs up when he was forced to snap his head to look at the field, hearing the scream of a player in agonising pain. "No, it can't be, not Sebastian!"

The whistle blew for half-time break, and the team carried Sebastian from the field to the locker room. "What will we do now, Coach?"

The coach answered, "We can't change the game plan now. We have a lead of twenty points, so we stick to the plan because the plan is working."

Just like in sports, businesses sometimes need to alter their game plan when situations change. Pivoting is common in the startup world when original assumptions prove flawed. Successful pivots require analysing warning signs, understanding your phase of growth, and adapting strategies while staying true to your core mission.

Back at the rugby game, the whistle blew, and the second half was in play. The team secured the ball and the nine, as told, does not kick but pass the ball to the standing in fly-half. He missed his mark because the new fly-half was not standing where Sebastian would have stood. The team started to crumble, and Coach Nick started making changes to the game plan, "Kick the ball number 9," but he did not practice at all this season. He kicked the ball directly into touch, and the opposition had the line out; they attacked and scored.

The final whistle blew, and Coach Nick's team lost the game by one point.

Sebastian's injury was assessed, and the doctor couldn't make a diagnosis of healing yet; maybe recovery would take one week or two. The team would have to wait for the results. The team prepared for the next game with the same game plan; after all, Sebastian might be ready to play. Come Saturday, Sebastian was not ready, and the team stuck to the game plan and failed. The second week, same process, and again Sebastian was not ready. The team stuck to the game plan and failed. The coach realised that Sebastian potentially wouldn't be returning, and he should rather change his game plan in anticipation of his non-return. Coach Nick re-assessed each team player's contribution and potential and made some positional changes. The game plan was now changed for the new team structure. On game day, Coach Nick finally got his win.

One thing that is certain in life is change, and there are sometimes uncontrollable events that can alter the way you have to do business. You could have written the best business model and understood each and every key activity within your business, but it does happen that an aspect of your business model gets disrupted. Sometimes the game plan starts off slow, but as the players gain experience and confidence, the game plan makes sense if you just stay true to it. The same is true with your business; if you believe in your value proposition and your game plan is focused on it, it might be slow business at first, but if you monitor and manage progression, it will reach a tipping point of success. But sometimes entrepreneurs are so focused on what they created or want to do that they are too stubborn to change the game plan in hopes that the tables will turn. Many do and reap the rewards; others don't and fail even when they have received advice that their game plan won't work.

WARNING SIGNS A PIVOT IS COMING

Are you just changing things and throwing spaghetti against the wall before you go to the second phase? Time has fast implications; it can either heal your business or completely destroy it. My wife's beauty business had all the potential in the world, but I did not have the means or finances to buy time or change my game plan. Maybe if I had the funding, it might have come to fruition; it might also not have. Your bank balance is normally a good indication if your business is working or has a forecasted cash flow sheet that you have to tweak and rework just to make the numbers work.

Notable startups like Twitter, Instagram, and Slack all pivoted successfully from struggling original ideas to the massive successes they are today. Twitter originally focused on podcasting before pivoting to microblogging. Instagram started as a location-based social app before transforming into photo sharing. Slack changed course from an online gaming platform to workplace communication. Assessing performance data gave them the conviction to change course.

THREE PHASES OF THE PIVOT

Knowing which phase your business is in allows you to set appropriate expectations around pivoting or staying the course. The maturation process typically follows three main phases, each with different considerations when assessing changes. In general, there are three phases when that could make you decide to get a strategic investor.

- Phase 1: In this phase, you make a plan. If you missed out on a lot of the points in the book, you are going to have to spend a lot of time deconstructing… so it might be better to start over.
- Phase 2: You have an investable business, but you might have to tweak one or two elements. You need to do the due diligence to identify which elements need change.
- Phase 3: You have the right plan, but the thought of cash flow gets overwhelming and thinking more corporate, and creating better processes is overwhelming. Maybe you fall out of love with the business. One of the things that makes this phase difficult to overcome is fear of the unknown.

In Phase 1, founders are still testing and iterating on their model. Pivoting here is expected as assumptions get validated. In Phase 2, core product-market fit is established but scaling may require adjustments. Pivots should be more incremental. By Phase 3, you have product-channel fit at scale. Only pivot if growth stalls for an extended period. Understand your current phase to set pivot expectations.

PIVOTING WITH PURPOSE

One of the things a lot of people tell me is they like the amount of patience I bring. Adam was a Phase 3. He had a profitable sole trader business making enough money to sustain his daily life. He had many opportunities to grow his business and every time he started exploring it, the thought of cash flow and scaling his business but knowing business principles was overwhelming; he was afraid of being in uncomfortable situations where he would panic and not know what to do, so it was easier to revert back to the simple model to do the job, charge what he thought it was worth, and get his income.

Many entrepreneurs resist pivoting even when signs point to a need for adaptation. With patient guidance, they can overcome the fear of the unknown and implement necessary strategic shifts.

I've talked in earlier chapters about Adam, the landscaping business owner who was directed to me through a mutual friend who he sought advice from. I have always had time for inspiring people who want to better themselves and within the very first coffee, he knew that if he wanted to grow, he needed not only cash flow but also an advisor and mentor.

Adam had good ideas, but money alone wouldn't put him in the right position to be able to fully execute on those ideas. He needed someone who could help him to help create the game plan for when a player gets injured, and he needed to pivot. One of the primary things smart money can bring to the business is the perspective of when to be calm enough to sit back, assess the situation, and rewrite the game plan if needed, or stick to the plan and always deliver.

Business, like sports, requires practice and adjustment. An effective pivot is not a random Hail Mary, but a strategic shift grounded in data. With the right mindset, planning, and analysis, pivots can lead to winning results.

11

YOU ARE THE PRODUCT

Our life *is* a business. There is a direct correlation between thinking of creating a business model or marketing your own business and creating a life model and marketing your own life. You, as an individual, are the product at the end of the day. Investors, and even your current workplace for that matter, invest in you as an individual.

Investors have needs and become the target market.

Your employees have needs so they become the target market.

How do you create the value proposition that gives you the best chance to fulfil those needs?

The business model you create matters, for sure, but the person you are as the executor of that business plan is going to have an even bigger effect on whether or not you can attract a strategic partner who can make this dream happen.

Whether you insource or outsource knowledge, or even just demonstrate that you understand basic business principles can set you apart from the rest, by just following all the steps we have explained within this book and applying it to yourself.

Just as with any new business approach, you have to understand your current value proposition. What are the strengths and opportunities you have to give and lay before you? What are the weaknesses and threats you have to work on or manage and eliminate?

WRITE YOUR OWN STORY

My mother was a very brave person. She was sixteen years old when I was born and gave up the opportunity of further education and a potential flourishing sporting career to take care of me. By the age of twenty, she already had three children. When I was ten years old, my mother and father got divorced. I effectively was raised by a single parent as my father would just disappear, and I only truly got to know him again when I was twenty years old. All this life pressure took a toll on my mother, and she resorted to comforting herself with alcohol to make it through the day.

Her drinking became a real problem and created a toxic environment that I just did not want to be a part of. I was just starting high school, and from a young age, I was very independent. I decided that I would go and visit my friends and arrange a sleepover. One night became two, which become three. After a week, my mother would eventually phone my mate's mother and ask if I was at their house. I found comfort in being in a stable environment, and I reckoned that if I could just abide by their house rules and make their family like me, they would not mind me staying.

Now, the reason I'm mentioning this is because this had a positive and negative effect on the perceived value proposition I created. On the negative side, being liked by my friends' family and peers became my goal, and so that long-lasting effect made me into a bit of a people-pleaser. There was a time in my history that I would agree to any situation or offer assistance to all around me just to be accepted or liked, fully knowing it would be near impossible to honour all these commitments. But as long as they liked me at that point in time, I knew I would be safe.

While this approach had a dark shadow, there were many benefits, as well, that shaped much of my success. You can't have the light without the dark. The trick is to learn to tame the dark, so it doesn't swallow the light.

ADAPT TO YOUR AUDIENCE

The experience of family surfing in my teens gave me the ability to change and adapt my reactions, behaviour, and tone of the discussion to suit the current atmosphere or client base. I can walk into a lawyer's office and be as formal as I need to be and, at the same time, have a business discussion with the local coffee shop owner in shorts and slacks.

Now I would not have known this if I hadn't followed the same process and principles of assessment and understanding the key activities that I would recommend my clients and other businesses to follow.

As I did a deep dive into my own personal life model, as my life is a business, it proved hard to differentiate emotion from reality. Most people are not critical or cynical of themselves. What works for me is to just write things down, not to think, not to ponder, and not to evaluate until I have stopped. Write down whatever is in your mind, without judgement and know there is no obligation to present pr to perform. This is a way of assessing your current belief and the value proposition you believe you are creating. Now that you know your current value proposition, you can identify the target market you want to present your value proposition to.

When I first immigrated to Australia, I was ready to fill any position; I knew that I just needed an in and knew that I had the capability to work myself through the ranks. My CV for me was a snapshot of my business model. I would carefully read and study what the needs are of the required company and would address my CV in the same manner. Now I did not lie on my CV, but just showing my understanding of what they wanted gave me the competitive edge.

Just as in business, you need to understand what will help you create or advance your current value proposition. Simply by being a human being, you do not have a niche market. The market you "serve" can range from direct family, such as your spouse and kids, to extended family members like your parents, siblings, or aunts and uncles. On top of that you, as a human being, you will have co-workers, a boss, peers, and, if you are a current business owner, your employees to serve. This is not a clear niche! These are a lot of different people with different demographics and different needs.

Your job, if you want to think about it this way, is to present your value proposition to your family, your peers, and, if you want to grow a business, your potential strategic investor.

Knowing your current value proposition and potential future value proposition is essential to getting what you want from any of the members of your "target market." What puts you in the driver's seat is to establish how you maintain or advance the creation of your value proposition. By the same token, you can establish how you execute your current or future value propositions.

So how do you create or advance your current personal value proposition?

Once you start thinking of yourself as the business, you can see how to apply the steps we have gone through in this book for your business and apply them to yourself as a person:

- Know your value.
- Know your customer.
- Know how to be a good customer.
- Focus on the right activities and track your progress.
- Optimise your cost structure.
- Create solid back up plans.

What is the value you bring to your circle of friends, family, and co-workers? How can you serve them so that in helping them get what they want, you get what you want? How can you effectively evaluate the key activities with your potential suppliers that affect your daily life and optimise the expenses and benefits?

In personal development, the focus is similar to a product and its research development program. You identify the key needs to research, design, and create. Once identified, you do not have the luxury to insource or outsource this need. You are the product; you fulfil the need.

You will have to explore the key activities that will help create or maintain your current value proposition; research and development should happen at least two hours once a week. For others, the time needed might be more. IT products, process, and development are one of the fastest knowledge-growing categories today. If you're an IT expert, today does not mean that you will be one tomorrow. If you're the only one who knows how to design an IT concept today and decide to make it a business, it does not mean you will own the intellectual property tomorrow.

The value you can offer will be different based on the needs of the people in your life. Your family needs can be your time. What are the key activities you have to put into place to create more time with your family? It's quite possible this part of your "market," your family, is looking to you for financial support. How can you optimise the time you spend with them and balance it with the financial support you need to provide to them? Is your current usage of time creating enough sustainable income to provide for your family's needs?

Just as in the business, you have to understand the value you are creating and who the customers are. How do you create or develop that value proposition?

CONTINUOUS DEVELOPMENT FUELS GROWTH

I truly believe that no minute spent reading a book, sitting in a seminar or classroom, or even just learning online is a waste of time. When we immigrated to Australia, my wife had security in my position as General Manager of Merchandise and Marketing of the biggest independent supermarket retail group. But my wife still wanted to contribute and set off to start her own business. I knew that this would be a great learning experience for her and stayed true to my philosophy that if you help others to get what they want, you will get what you want.

She saw an opportunity in online product marketing. Now, she knew nothing about online marketing, let alone website creation, maintenance, or how to link suppliers to your online portals. We just immigrated, and not having much disposable income, we could not afford to invest in marketing platforms to create or even maintain the websites. My wife took it upon herself to study how to create and build websites. It was very basic at first. As she explored multiple business ideas, she would change her mind of focus and decide to embark on a new trend and a new product to sell, but the distribution channel remained the same; she had to create a new website platform to promote her new idea and platforms. Now I think it is safe to say that within twenty-four months, she created endless numbers of different websites and platforms for herself, and every new one was more advanced than the previous.

Now many would have said she had failed, but I disagree with the sentiment. During all this time of exploring and trying to create online businesses, she managed to develop a skill set that allows her to be able to create any website or shopping platform. She can create online shopping portals linked to web accounts and now even knows how to integrate 3PL shipping companies into the model that will directly communicate to them from one platform to another. Can I remind you that she used to be a beauty therapist before this? All that time spent creating websites for short-lasting businesses was never a failure, it was a learning platform she chose to insource the skill, and today she is a marketing manager specialising in creating and maintaining all website and social marketing needs. She still has her own online business in designing and handcrafting beautiful earrings, so her entrepreneurial passion never died, it just took a different form than she might have expected. This is the journey of entrepreneurship when you realise at the end of the day it is *you* that is the real product.

And there is one last irony here I need to share with you. You are not only the product; you are the customer as well. In life, you not only need to know your value, create and execute the plan, and optimise your performance, you must also fundamentally fulfil a need in yourself with the work you do. If you give what you are getting, what are your needs? Do you just need a business that can support and maintain your lifestyle, or are you a big-picture thinker who wants to create and build an empire? Your life model must be focused on whatever you want the outcome to be because you can't just execute the plan, the plan has to serve your goals and dreams. This is the challenge and the benefit of being an entrepreneur. Owning a business gives you more levers to pull to serve your customers – not just in business but in your life, and one of those customers, at the end of the day, is you.

12

DOING IT ANYWAY

If every person who ever thought of opening a business was able to do so, there most likely would not be anyone left to do the work. There are so many people who love the idea of sustaining themselves or being the masters of their own destiny but just never get around to do it. It took me the loss of my loved ones to wake up; even though I had the same passion and some sort of motivation, it was way easier just to go on with life and not break the barriers of facing the demons that stood in my way.

OVERCOMING FEAR AND SELF-DOUBT

The reality is that even though you have read through this book and empowered yourself to take the next step, that does not mean that you will actually make it. You are the sum total of the choices that you make and it's the small choices that you will be making from now on that will shape your future. And unfortunately, no one can do it for you because you have to do it yourself. You have to remember that tomorrow is promised to no one; there might not be a next day to start taking action, so live today to the fullest.

Starting a new business takes a lot of sacrifices. You might have to sacrifice some time with your family but it's all about the quality of time that you spend with them and not the quantity. Think about the potential extra time you might get to enjoy with them if you do succeed. You might also have to sacrifice your current lifestyle. You have to have the lowest possible running cost that your cash flow allows so starting with big salaries might just set you up for failure. But remember why you are doing this in the first place. Never lose sight of the reward. You have to feel it and imagine it but do not get stuck on it. You might even be funding your lifestyle already so show that, but the incremental value will be amazing. Quantify your lifestyle, is your current lifestyle a lifestyle you want or *need?* Can you scale it back in the short term by reducing your lifestyle? Investors will appreciate that personal sacrifice.

If you can't cut your lifestyle in the meantime, then it might not be the right time for you to embark on this journey. When you're in this mindset it is hard to manage cash flow in your business. When I first emigrated to Australia, my wife and I were starting almost from scratch. We needed to develop social networks, build up our savings again (international moves are expensive), and learn a whole new culture. It just wasn't the right time for me to be in a high-risk, new entrepreneurial venture. It's not always the right time. Having a steady paycheck at that point in my life was one of the best decisions I could make for what would later become my next business.

I have seen it before where business owners will see their business cash flow as income and splurges, and then two to three weeks later, they are broke, then money flows in again, and they splurge again, and so the cycle continues. Those individuals have to figure out what their true expenses are and put them on a manageable salary base, including cash flow. Salary can be more sustainable through the highs and lows. Even if it's lower. Is there a way you can set up a salary for yourself to have a meaningful lifestyle but still maintain cash flow?

TURNING WANTS INTO MUSTS

One of the barriers I often see is the idea that "I don't know enough" or "I'm not good enough." There is this notion of rank and power; you are only as good as you think you are, but I remember a story from my studies of a school teacher who teaches first grade students. To these students, she is the cleverest, most powerful person they know, but then this same teacher will go on lunch break with the headmaster, and she sees him as the one with rank, and she gives away her power. That headmaster used to be a teacher. Imagine if he also said, "I'm not good enough or don't know enough." Every one of us thinks that others know more than us or others are better than us, so just remember that there are people who think *you* know more than them or *you* are better than them.

It's very daunting getting started. You might feel like, "I won't do it today and will think about it tomorrow." Because that creates procrastination. You can't start and not finish. The lack of accountability is a big deal as well. This is where a strategic investment partner adds surprising value; you know you will have someone who is asking questions and will even begin to expect what those questions will be and do extra work to be prepared for them.

When you sit back and expect other people to do the work for you, you miss out on the opportunity to learn from the process. I had to go and be the store manager to really understand the problems managers face. I was not a store manager forever, but if I didn't do the job, I wouldn't have learnt what I needed to know to build the right company. Another example is someone who hates sales, not wanting to do sales because of a fear of rejection. But you can't expect someone else to sell it if *you* can't sell it.

One should not fear rejection or be ashamed of it, as rejection teaches valuable lessons and makes one qualified. I overcame that same fear for example. For an instant, I thought about what the people with bigger businesses or bigger investment portfolios might think, "Who am I to write this book?" But for me, the way I move forward is by turning my wants into musts. Once I decide I am going to do something, failure is not an option. It becomes my most important task, and other things fall off my priority list. If I keep moving forward towards the goal, I will be there tomorrow. Tomorrow becomes today, and then tomorrow becomes today, and the cycle continues. That is how I create momentum.

For me, the fear of *not* doing something is greater than *not* knowing I tried to the best of my ability to be the best version of myself. Live life with no regrets and take calculated risks. Don't just jump into the first best thing; instead, never stop exploring. You will find that opportunity to take action. I feel sad for people wishing for things when they haven't tried to achieve their dreams. I wish I could share my joy with them to make them see what they potentially could be missing out on – not my success but theirs.

LEADING BY EXAMPLE

One of the things that personally motivates me to get through moments of fear is the example I want to set for my daughter, Miané. I believe children learn what they live, and I hope that seeing her father push to be the best version of himself will inspire her to live her own life to its full potential.

If you *want* a strategic investor for your idea, but you aren't willing to take the risk of doing all this work and failing yourself, how can you ask an investor to risk their money on it? I had the privilege to see so many people grow right in front of me, and so many times they would reflect on where they came from and not one of them ever regretted taking the first step, whether they succeeded or not.

Live your life with gusto and enthusiasm.

13

WITH GUSTO

Gusto means enthusiasm, excitement, energy, and happiness. The happiness doesn't *just* come from the result but from the process of getting to that result. As we reach the end of this journey, walking through the Building a Business with Gusto framework, I hope you feel empowered with new skills, knowledge, and perspective to chart your own path to entrepreneurial success. Crafting a compelling vision is exhilarating, but implementing it in the real world is never straightforward. The inevitable twists and turns can leave you disoriented unless you have a guiding light to stay centred on true north. This book provides that illuminated roadmap based on lessons learnt over decades of hands-on experience, mistakes made, and wisdom gained. At the core, success stems from understanding your competitive position thoroughly first, not from overestimating potential. Letting passion outpace practical planning is a common pitfall.

An idea is only as strong as the business model, execution strategy, and defensible advantages backing it up.

ACHIEVE YOUR GREATNESS

By now, you recognise that attracting smart money starts with demonstrating your value. Analyse your strengths, weaknesses, opportunities, and threats to take stock of your current position. Calculate costs and efficiencies to showcase profit drivers credibly. Uncover sustainable competitive advantages. With compelling substantiation, investors can clearly evaluate the opportunity and projected returns. You also understand why partnering with the right investment partner is pivotal. Assess your capital and expertise gaps to determine if you need funds alone or hands-on guidance. Strategic investors accelerate growth through capital, networks, and oversight to steer major decisions. But silent investors allow greater autonomy if you have confidence in your team. Vet investor fit based on your skills needs. Creating and delivering a value proposition that aligns target customers and channels streamlines your model. Avoid dilution from trying to be everything to everyone. Define your core segments and tailor messaging and channels accordingly. Supplier relationships directly impact product experience and margins, so help them succeed too.

Staying focused on essential activities multiplies your efforts. Prioritise based on value creation and assign ownership. Revisit often as business cycles through phases. Pivoting with purpose, not randomly, adapts your model to capitalise on change. Vigilance on costs differentiates viable businesses as they scale. Analyse fixed versus variable cost projections at projected volumes. Optimising COGS and "make versus buy" decisions demonstrates the business acumen investors seek. But you alone bring the magic. View yourself as both the entrepreneurial product and the customer. Clarify your personal and professional goals, strengths and needs. Never stop developing relevant skills. Help others succeed on their journeys, and they'll return the favour.

This framework synthesises the collaboration of leading with gusto and planning with prudence. But book knowledge alone is not power – it merely creates potential power. True power springs from implementing these concepts deliberately, consistently, and energetically over time. I wish you great success in bringing your own vision to life. Stay determined when doubts creep in. The world needs what you have to offer.

TOMORROW IS NOT PROMISED

Now that you've reached the summit, take a moment to survey the terrain from this hard-earned vantage point. Enjoy a deep breath of fresh optimism while looking down the slopes you've climbed. But don't linger long – your next peak awaits. With the resilience you've forged, I have no doubt you will thrive on the path ahead.

In this book, you learnt the framework of the seven

principles of the Build a Business with Gusto framework, but the gusto part has to come from inside you. Don't take the wrong investor. Don't build a business that is going to imprison you. You have to know what you are getting into. Whatever you are taking on today, do it with success in mind. Life changes. Tomorrow isn't promised. You can change your mind later but be focused. Don't let fear stop you from achieving greatness and achieving who you want to be. All of us are valuable. Most people who you see as successful started small, and they kept going. My wish for you as you finish this book is that you keep going and find that smart money that will change your life, your business, and maybe even the world forever.

ACKNOWLEDGMENTS

I am so blessed with so many people who contributed to my life so I could become who I am today. I cannot think of a single person who I had a relationship with who did not contribute in some way, and I will forever be grateful to them all. My first book is so dear to me. It's my first steppingstone to self-fulfillment and very emotional; emotions are created and shared with the home I grew in and the one I created. These are the special people who are currently in my life and also those who no longer are.

To my wife and daughter,
They say home is where the heart is, and it could not have been truer with you both in my life. You have created a haven with unconditional love and support regardless of the sacrifice and cost it might bring. You allow me to live a life with Gusto where I can stretch my boundaries and be the man I'm destined to be. I know that together we will be able to overcome any crossroads we might face and that makes me fearless.

Lecinda, I cannot be more honoured to be called your husband. I still remember the day when we were just six months together and the banks came to take my cars back; I have not been more embarrassed in my life, but your words on that day have always stuck by me. "I am not with you for your money but the potential you see in yourself." Every day I strive to live up to that potential you see in me, and I know it is just not financial but also being a great husband as well. Your love for me shines out of you every day and a man could not have asked for better. I hold on to the words that got prophesised over me that I will spread the word of God in business and that he would send me a wife. I did not know what he was talking about because I was single at that time, and five days later I met you. You are God sent.

Miané, my beautiful daughter. You're the reason I believe in God and angels. You are such a blessing in my life, and you are so blessed with wisdom, charisma, and talent. Sometimes it is almost seeing a mini me growing up before my eyes. You are destined for greatness and may I be blessed enough to be able to sow into your life and be a part of it. You make me proud to be a father and your cuddles every day keeps me going, living life with Gusto.

Love you both forever.

To my late brothers,

There is not a day that goes by that your influence in my life does not shine through. I think of you constantly and both of your passings can seem so senseless but know that both of you are happy and loved where you are. I really wish we had more time together; especially now, I have so much to give and would have been an honour to be part of your lives.

Micheal,

We have not spoken a word to each other since your birth, but I know that you could understand me and you always smiled as you recognised my voice. Your disability for many would have been a barrier but for me it made you the special person that you were, and you had so many people who took care of you and loved you and that says a lot. Even though your young death was always a possibility, it does not make it easier to have said goodbye.

Christo,

I never said it enough, but I love you and am proud of you. When I was going on my life journey, you were the one who took care of the people at home and took up responsibilities that you never should have. Today I so wish that I was there for you more in a way of support and guidance. In your last couple of years, you really did become a great young man and saw the eagerness in your eyes to grow as a person and take on the world. Your death was so unexpected and at the age of twenty-five you still had so much potential and still so much to do. Your death is why I'm living a life with Gusto; it is not the kick I wanted but it is the gift your death gave me.

Rest in peace my brothers and know that you will always be in my heart.

To my late mother,

Words cannot express my gratitude of all the things you have done for me. At a tender young age, you had me, and your life was not easy, yet you never made me experience the pain and hardship you endured. For a big part of your life, you had to be a single mother and you were a super mother. I still remember my school lunch boxes full of the nicest sandwiches filled with steak and garnish or the sausage rolls that had to be packed in a used ice cream container because it would not fit in a normal lunch box, even though I sold it to my classmates or exchanged it for sweets.

Your sacrifices were only understood by me so late in my life with my own daughter being born. You worked ten-hour days and sold of your leave time so that we can be taken care of. We were always your number one priority and hope I will be able to mirror that.

Now you are with both your sons in Heaven, and I can see you all running together in the gardens of Eden. I will love you forever.

 Greg Weiss is a serial entrepreneur, business advisor, and strategic investor based in Australia. With over twenty-four years of experience in the supermarket industry, Greg has spearheaded upgrades, renovations, and new store builds for retail chains in South Africa and Australia.

After immigrating to Australia in 2017, Greg served as general manager for a champion supermarket group, overseeing over 100 stores and 9,000 employees. In this role, he focused on strategic analysis to set organisational direction and build execution systems. His goal has always been helping independent retailers and large corporations alike build better businesses. Greg's experience across the full supermarket supply chain, in both wholesale and retail, gives him unique insights into end-to-end value creation.

In 2019, he established the advisory firm Live Life with Gusto, serving entrepreneurs and investors. He has recently founded new supermarket, landscaping, and transport ventures, applying his strategic expertise.

Greg holds an MBA from Stellenbosch Business

School and is passionate about sustainable partnerships and business model innovation. Through his writing, speaking, and advising, Greg aims to equip aspiring entrepreneurs with the skills to attract strategic capital and build thriving businesses.

ABOUT DIFFERENCE PRESS

Difference Press is the publishing arm of The Author Incubator, an Inc. 500 award-winning company that helps business owners and executives grow their brand, establish thought leadership, and get customers, clients, and highly-paid speaking opportunities, through writing and publishing books.

While traditional publishers require that you already have a large following to guarantee they make money from sales to your existing list, our approach is focused on using a book to grow your following – even if you currently don't have a following. This is why we charge an up-front fee but never take a percentage of revenue you earn from your book.

☞ MORE THAN A COACH. MORE THAN A PUBLISHER. ✍

We work intimately and personally with each of our authors to develop a revenue-generating strategy for the book. By using a Lean Startup style methodology, we guarantee the book's success before we even start writing. We provide all the technical support authors need with editing, design, marketing, and publishing, the emotional support you would get from a book coach to help you manage anxiety and time constraints, and we serve as a strategic thought partner engineering the book for success.

The Author Incubator has helped almost 2,000 entrepreneurs write, publish, and promote their non-fiction books. Our authors have used their books to gain international media exposure, build a brand and marketing following, get lucrative speaking engagements, raise awareness of their product or service, and attract clients and customers.

☞ ARE YOU READY TO WRITE A BOOK? ✍

As a client, we will work with you to make sure your book gets done right and that it gets done quickly. The Author Incubator provides one-stop for strategic book consultation, author coaching to manage writer's block and anxiety, full-service professional editing, design, and self-publishing services, and book marketing and launch campaigns. We sell this as one package so our clients are not slowed down with contradictory advice. We have a 99 percent success rate with nearly all of our clients completing their books, publishing them, and reaching bestseller status upon launch.

☞ APPLY NOW AND BE OUR NEXT SUCCESS STORY ✍

To find out if there is a significant ROI for you to write a book, get on our calendar by completing an application at www.TheAuthorIncubator.com/apply.

OTHER BOOKS BY DIFFERENCE PRESS

The Favor Factor: Achieve Career Advancement and Financial Success Using Universal Laws by Lacheena Carothers

Ascending in Scrubs: How Nurses Triumph over Burnout to Manifest Their Dream by. N. Collins-Clagett, BSN, RN

Fundraising without Burnout: Radically Reimagining Philanthropy to Transform Your Impact by Radha Friedman

Diagnosis Concussion: Your Essential Guide to Holistic Healing, Recovery, and Returning to a Joyful Life by Amy Coughlin Greene

Focus Pocus: A Parent's Guide to Fostering Concentration, Resilience, and Academic Achievement in a Distracted World by Nancy Howes, MEd

Art of the Heart: The Doctor-Patient Partnership by Jay H. Kleiman, MD

Prove Them Wrong: One Immigrant's 10-Year Journey from Bankrupt to Millionaire by Héctor E. Quiroga, J.D.

Team Turnaround: Spark High Performance in Your Direct Reports by Lisa C. Shumpert

Senior Seeking Soulmate: The Master Plan for Finding Meaningful Companionship by Dr. Charlene Inman Smith

THANK YOU

It has been such an honour to have you read this book and to share the limited but useful information that I had the privilege to share with you. It is always hard to get the full picture on pages and you can find yourself typing endless information and still not being able to answer all your questions. I will most definitely write more books soon that might be able to answer what you are seeking.

So, to be able to assist you now and to say thank you for putting your trust in me, I will give you a free high-level assessment of your business idea, or assist if you seek clarity on the next step of your current business situation. Submit your enquiry to www.livewgusto.com and reference the book subtitle – *how to find strategic investors* – in your submission. On this site you will also gain free access to podcasts and information that will give you better insight into the world of entrepreneurship and building a business with gusto.

In addition to the website you can find valuable information by following me on social media:

- Facebook: www.facebook.com/livewgusto
- Instagram: www.instagram.com/livewgusto
- X: www.twitter.com/livewgusto

www.ingramcontent.com/pod-product-compliance
Lightning Source LLC
Chambersburg PA
CBHW060105260726
48658CB00004B/1406